First Dinosaur Encyclopedia

DK PUBLISHING

DK

LONDON, NEW YORK,
MELBOURNE, MUNICH, and DELHI

Written and edited by Caroline Bingham
Design team Jane Tetzlaff, Tory Gordon-Harris,
Clare Harris, Claire Patane, Mary Sandberg
Helen Chapman, Kath Northam

Publishing Manager Susan Leonard
Art Director Rachael Foster
Category Publisher Mary Ling
Picture Researcher Liz Moore
DK Picture Library Rose Horridge,
Claire Bowers
Production Controller Lucy Baker
DTP Designer Emma Hansen-Knarhoi
Jacket Designer Karen Hood
US Editor Margaret Parrish
Consultant Dougal Dixon B.SC. (Hons.), M.SC

First published in the United States in 2007
by DK Publishing
375 Hudson Street
New York, New York 10014

07 08 09 10 11 10 9 8 7 6 5 4 3 2 1
Copyright © 2007 Dorling Kindersley Limited

DK books are available at special discounts when purchases in bulk
for sales promotions, premiums, fundraising, or educational use.
For details, contact: DK Publishing Special Markets,
375 Hudson Street, New York, New York 10014
SpecialSales@dk.com

A catalog record for this book
is available from the Library of Congress.
ISBN 978-0-7566-2814-7

Color reproduction by Colourscan, Singapore
Printed and bound by Toppan, China

Discover more at
www.dk.com

Contents

Introduction

Let's look at dinosaurs

Triassic dinosaurs

There is a question at the bottom of each page...

Baby *T. rex* may have been covered in fur.

About this book

The pages of this book have special features that will show you how to get your hands on as much information as possible! Look out for these:

The **Curiosity quiz** will get you searching through each section for the answers.

Become an expert tells you where to look for more information on a subject.

Every page is color-coded to show you which section it is in.

weird or what? These buttons give extra weird and wonderful facts.

Age of the dinosaurs

Earth has an incredibly long history, as it formed about 4.6 billion years ago. Geologists divide the passage of time since into eras. Dinosaurs lived in the Mesozoic Era.

A question of time
Different dinosaurs lived at different times, and many of the best-known dinosaurs never actually met. *T. rex* and *Stegosaurus* never fought because their existence was separated by about 80 million years.

MESOZOIC ERA

Eoraptor
See page 42

Plateosaurus
See page 38

See page 46

Brachiosaurus
See page 51

Stegosaurus
See page 28

Triassic: 248 to 206 million years ago   Jurassic: 206 to 144 million years ago

How do we know what dinosaurs looked like?

Albertosaurus was a Cretaceous dinosaur.

The Mesozoic Era

This era is divided into three time spans, or periods:

The **Cretaceous** period was ruled by an amazing variety of dinosaurs.

The **Jurassic** period saw the emergence of massive plant-eating dinosaurs.

The **Triassic** period, the oldest, saw the appearance of Earth's first dinosaurs.

Geological time is always shown with the oldest period at the bottom of the list. It reflects the sequence in which rocks are laid down.

Giganotosaurus
See page 78

Velociraptor
See page 84

T. rex
See page 76

Human beings (homo sapiens) didn't appear until very recently in Earth's history.

Homo sapiens

Cretaceous: 144 to 65 million years ago

Curiosity quiz

Look through the Age of the dinosaurs pages to identify each of the picture clues below.

Become an expert

on where *Albertosaurus* roamed, pages **68–69**

5

We know a lot about their size and appearance from fossil evidence.

The "terrible lizard"

Prof. Richard Owen (1804–1892) with the skeleton of a moa, an extinct flightless bird.

Scientists once believed dinosaur fossils were the bones of a type of lizard. In fact, the word "dinosaur" means "terrible lizard." "Dinosaur" was first used in 1841.

A starting point

When Richard Owen first coined the term "dinosaur," only three of the creatures had been identified: *Iguanodon*, *Megalosaurus*, and *Hylaeosaurus*.

Lizard

It's the same one!

Is it two-footed or four? Where does that spiked part go? Ideas about dinosaurs change over the years, as these portrayals of *Iguanodon* show.

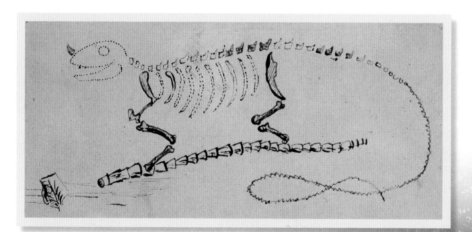

The first sketch of *Iguanodon* had a spike positioned on its snout.

6

Was *Iguanodon* a plant-eater or a meat-eater?

Where in the world?

From sparse beginnings, dinosaurs have now been found on every continent, including the frozen wastes of Antarctica. This map gives an idea of where just a few dinosaur remains have been found.

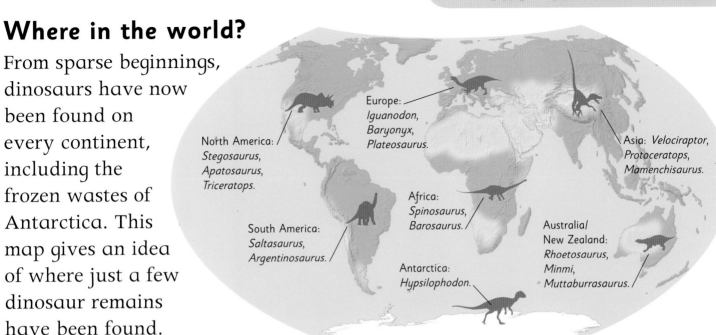

Europe: *Iguanodon, Baryonyx, Plateosaurus.*

North America: *Stegosaurus, Apatosaurus, Triceratops.*

Asia: *Velociraptor, Protoceratops, Mamenchisaurus.*

Africa: *Spinosaurus, Barosaurus.*

South America: *Saltasaurus, Argentinosaurus.*

Australia/ New Zealand: *Rhoetosaurus, Minmi, Muttaburrasaurus.*

Antarctica: *Hypsilophodon.*

Iguanodon

In the 1850s, a sculpture of *Iguanodon* showed a lizard crawling on its belly.

The name *Iguanodon* means "iguana toothed." The teeth were like those of the iguana, the modern, plant-eating lizard.

We now know that *Iguanodon* had spikes on its thumbs, not on its nose.

Scientists believe that *Iguanodon* could walk on four feet, as well as on two.

Become an expert on what a dinosaur is, pages 14–15

It was a plant-eater.

A very different Earth

Earth is constantly changing. Today, there are seven continents, but the first dinosaurs lived on one giant supercontinent called Pangaea.

A moving jigsaw
Earth's crust is made up of sections, called plates, which are always on the move. Continents rest on the plates. Over time, this movement changes the shape of the land.

It's breaking up

During the late Triassic period, Pangaea began to break up to form two supercontinents. By the end of the Cretaceous period the landmasses had undergone huge changes. From space, Earth would have looked more like it does today, with large continents separated by gigantic oceans.

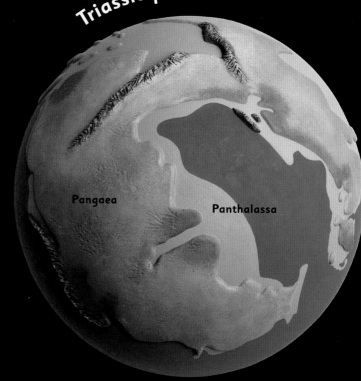

Pangaea

Panthalassa

The Triassic period saw the world's land all joined together as a supercontinent.

What are the names of Earth's seven continents?

We're free to roam

The existence of one huge landmass meant that in the early to mid-Triassic period animals and plants were similar throughout the world.

Pangaea means "All Earth."

What was different?

Pangaea's world had no ice caps and land life was hot and dry; large areas of desert dominated the center of this vast continent.

Jurassic period

Laurasia

Tethys sea

Gondwana

The landmass split apart in the Jurassic period, forming two huge continents.

Cretaceous period

India

Africa

Antarctica

The landmasses we know today began to appear during the Cretaceous period.

Africa, Asia, Australia, Antarctica, North America, South America, and Europe.

What did they see?

The dinosaurs looked out on to a very different world from the one we see today. It was a world without roads, houses, parks, power lines, and all the machines humans use. So what was it like?

Iguanodon

Habitat

Like us, the dinosaurs lived in different habitats. A habitat is an area that animals and plants share. It may be a desert or a busy city street.

Iguanodon was a plant-eater. By the time Iguanodon lived, the first flowering plants had appeared.

How many different types of grasses are there today?

From Triassic forests...

The first dinosaurs saw only brown and green—there were no flowering plants. Giant forests contained trees that were similar to plants we know today, only larger.

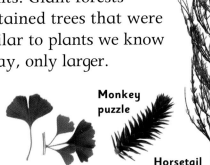

Triassic scene   Cycad

Ginkgo leaves

Monkey puzzle

Horsetail

... to Cretaceous flowers

The first flowering plants, such as magnolias and passion flowers, appeared in the Cretaceous period. By the late Cretaceous, there were also buttercups.

Magnolia

Fossilized dinosaur dung (coprolite)

Fossilized grass remains were found in dinosaur dung.

What about grass?

Until recently, scientists believed grass evolved after the dinosaurs, but there's now proof that some dinosaurs did eat grass. And it may have been grass that was several yards tall!

Buttercup

Dinosaur habitats

The dinosaurs enjoyed a huge variety of habitats, much as we do today.

 Deserts Large areas of desert were common in the Mesozoic Era.

 Forests Triassic trees were protected from over-browsing by tough needles.

 Mountains These increasingly appeared in the Mesozoic Era.

 Scrubland There were huge areas of scrubby, drought-resistant plants.

 Swampland Cretaceous swamps were good places for fossil preservation.

 Riverbanks Triassic dinosaurs stayed close to coasts or riverbanks.

The Cretaceous saw an increasing variety of flowers.

There are about 10,000 different types.

Let's look at dinosaurs

Large... small... meat-eater... plant-eater... There was an incredible variety of dinosaurs and we will probably never know just how many different kinds there were.

Sauropods such as Barosaurus were the largest animals ever.

Barosaurus

T. rex

I've got that!

Dinosaurs had plenty of features in common. They all had:

Scaly skin—Feathers may also have covered the bodies of some dinosaurs.

Long tails—used for balance and as a whip to fight off enemies.

Legs—held straight under the body.

Claws—whether meat-eater or plant-eater, all had claws.

Lesothosaurus

The very first dinosaurs, such as Lesothosaurus, were all small.

Larger dinosaurs, such as Stegosaurus, came later.

12

How long did dinosaurs live?

How many dinosaurs?

Scientists think there may have been at least 1,500 different dinosaur types, and probably many more. We know of about 550 that can be confirmed as distinct types, so there are a lot more to discover.

Curiosity quiz

Look through the Let's look at dinosaurs pages to identify each of the picture clues below.

Sauropods

Triceratops

Triceratops means "three-horned face."

How are they named?

Dinosaurs are usually named after the person who found them, after their features, or after the place they were found.

Stegosaurus

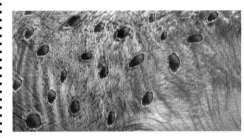

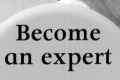

Become an expert

on *T. rex*, pages 76–77

on *Triceratops*, pages 72–73

No one knows. Some may have lived for 200 years.

What is a dinosaur?

Two legs or four? Meat-eater or plant-eater? What made a dinosaur? They all had four limbs, though many walked on two. There were a number of other features they had in common.

Giganotosaurus

Long tails
Scientists believe dinosaurs held their tails above the ground since there is no evidence of drag marks when tracks have been found.

Scaly skin
Impressions of dinosaur skin are rare, but paleontologists have found enough to know that dinosaurs had scaly skin, a little like crocodiles today.

Meat-eating dinosaurs were known as therapods.

Cold-blooded lizards have to warm up in sunlight; they cannot control their temperature.

All dinosaurs lived on land. They could not fly or swim.

Were dinosaurs warm-blooded?
It's possible that meat-eating dinosaurs were warm-blooded (like we are), while plant-eating sauropods were cold-blooded. Warm-blooded animals use food as fuel to stay warm. Sauropods were too large to have eaten enough to do this.

14

Are dinosaurs lizards?

Giganotosaurus skulls had huge "windows."

Skull holes

Dinosaur skulls had large holes, or "windows." These made them lighter, which was necessary since some of the largest skulls were almost as long as a car.

Meat-eaters had sharp claws.

Plant-eaters had blunt toenails.

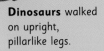

Clue in the claws

Meat-eating dinosaurs were known as theropods, which means "beast-footed," because they had sharp, hooked claws on their toes. Plant-eating dinosaurs tended to have blunt hooves or toenails.

Straight legs

Dinosaurs walked on their toes with their legs directly under their bodies.

Dinosaurs walked on upright, pillarlike legs.

Crocodiles stand with their knees and elbows slightly bent.

Lizards sprawl, with their knees and elbows held at right angles to their bodies.

Egg layers

All dinosaurs laid eggs—some in nests, just as birds do today. The baby developed in the egg until it was ready to hatch. About 40 kinds of dinosaur egg have been discovered.

No. They are related, but the two groups are different.

A hip question

Dinosaurs can be split into two groups, according to their hip bones: the saurischians (the lizard-hipped dinosaurs) and the orinithischians (or bird-hipped dinosaurs).

Bird-hipped dinosaurs had two pairs of hip bones pointing back.

Did *T. rex* and   *Triceratops* ever meet?

Most lizard-hipped dinosaurs had a pair of hip bones that pointed forward or down.

T. rex

Triceratops

weird or what?
Strangely enough, scientists believe that birds have evolved from lizard-hipped dinosaurs—not bird-hipped dinosaurs as you might expect!

Saurischians

All meat-eating dinosaurs were lizard-hipped, but some plant-eaters were also lizard-hipped. *T. rex* was lizard-hipped, but so was the mighty plant-eating *Diplodocus*, whom you will meet on page 50.

I'm in this group!

Saurischians can be divided into two main groups:

 Theropods, the meat-eaters, such as *Dilophosaurus*.

 Sauropodomorphs, such as *Brachiosaurus*, with their small heads and long necks.

Ornithischians

These were all plant-eaters. The swept-back bones allowed more room for the digestive organs, and meant their bellies could be carried toward the back, allowing some to walk or run away from danger on two legs.

I'm in that group!

Ornithischians can be divided into three main groups:

 Thyreophorans, the four-footed, armor-plated dinosaurs (e.g., *Stegosaurus*).

 Marginocephalians, who had heads with bony frills or horns (e.g., *Triceratops*).

 Ornithopods, the two-legged plant-eaters (e.g., *Iguanodon*).

Yes. There's evidence that *T. rex* preyed on *Triceratops*.

From little to big

Not all dinosaurs were giants, as is often believed. The smaller dinosaurs, such as *Oviraptor*, would have barely reached up to the large plant-eaters' ankles!

Long in the tooth?

Most dinosaurs had teeth, but size varied.

Human molars are used for grinding food before it is swallowed.

Ankylosaurs had small, ridged teeth for slicing up plant matter.

Sauropods had long, peglike teeth!

Thigh bone from a *Brachiosaurus.*

A human snack

It's difficult to imagine how large dinosaurs grew. Just look at this picture of a fossilized skull from a dinosaur that roamed the Sahara Desert 90 million years ago.

Carcharodontosaurus skull from the mid-Cretaceous period.

From small...

Some dinosaurs are best described as tiny, such as the rabbit-sized *Micropachycephalosaurus.* Its lengthy name means "tiny, thick-headed lizard."

Micropachycephalosaurus

... to dog-sized

The meat-eating *Oviraptor* was about 6 ft 6 in (2 m) from snout to tail. This dinosaur had an oddly shaped toothless beak.

Oviraptor lived in the Gobi Desert in Mongolia about 80 million years ago.

Oviraptor

Which were the biggest dinosaurs?

The big ones were really huge!

Antarctosaurus

Become an expert

on *Oviraptor*, page **23**

on sauropods, pages **50–53**

Antarctosaurus was probably unable to lift its head much above shoulder height.

... to truck-sized

The large plant-eaters, the sauropods, were massive. *Antarctosaurus* was about 60 ft (18 m) long and would have towered over you. Other plant-eaters may have been larger still. Experts believe that large sauropods ate enough plants every day to equal the weight of a small car.

The sauropods.

Find a friend

Many male animals today compete to win a mate. Stags crash their antlers together, while birds display colorful feathers. Scientists believe dinosaurs had to compete in similar ways.

What did they do?

Dinosaurs may have used their head crests to show off, just like a peacock uses its colorful tail feathers.

Corythosaurus

Courtship displays tell females which males are strong and are likely to make healthy young.

Peacock

Pachycephalosaurus

This dinosaur had bony spikes on its head and snout.

Bone head

Pachycephalosaurus's head was 2 ft 7 in (80 cm) long. The dome was made of solid bone as thick as a bowling ball.

Pachycephalosaurus skull

Fighting fit

During the breeding season, male *Pachycephalosaurus* may have butted each other in fights over females. Their backbones were adapted to absorb shock.

Where did *Pachycephalosaurus* live?

Did they talk?

Nobody knows if dinosaurs made sounds, but we suspect they did. *Parasaurolophus*, a hadrosaur, may have done this by blowing air through its crest.

Become an expert on crested hadrosaurs, pages **70–71**

Lambeosaurus skull

Parasaurolophus skull

Hypacrosaurus skull

Other hadrosaurs had different-shaped crests, suggesting they made different sounds.

Parasaurolophus

Brachylophosaurus

Talk like a frog

Brachylophosaurus had a short, solid crest. It may have had an inflatable pouch on the outside of this that could be used to make noises, a little like a frog's throat pouch.

Throat pouch

In the forests of North America.

21

Eggstraordinary eggs

Scientists have been lucky enough to find lots of fossilized dinosaur eggs, and even nests. There is a huge variety of sizes and shapes, from small, circular eggs that would fit into the palm of your hand to eggs the size of cannonballs.

The biggest?

Macroelongatoolithus xixiaensis is the largest known dinosaur egg. These massive eggs have been found in China and are thought to have been from a *Therizinosaur*.

This dinosaur egg fossil is from Mongolia.

A muddy home

Some eggs were laid in mud, which proved a perfect base for fossilization. Many nests were laid out in a spiral pattern.

Shaped like an egg?

Some dinosaur eggs were round, but others were elongated, rather like a loaf of bread.

This is a hen's egg: it shows just how large the *Therizinosaur* egg was.

Oviraptor egg nest from China, showing the eggs laid in a spiral pattern. Each egg is approximately 6 in (16 cm) long.

Were dinosaur egg shells soft and leathery like those of snakes?

Fossilized dinosaur egg

I'm making a break for it!

A tiny dinosaur hatchling breaks out of its egg casing. While some dinosaurs were probably ready to look after themselves after hatching, others would have depended on parental help for food and protection.

This is a model of a *Parasaurolophus* hatchling.

Oviraptor

Egg

Egg care?

Did dinosaurs sit on their eggs, like birds today? We know that some did; this *Oviraptor* died and was fossilized while sitting on her nest of eggs some 80 million years ago.

Become an expert

on parental care of young dinosaurs, pages 24–25

Oviraptor

Nest is dug out of sand or dirt.

Bringing it back to life

This model re-creates the fossilized scene above, showing the *Oviraptor* shielding her eggs. *Oviraptors* had strange-looking beaked snouts. They may have raided other nests for food for themselves and their young.

No. They had hard, brittle shells, like the eggs of birds.

Birth and care of young

We know that some dinosaurs lived in colonies, thanks to finds of fossilized mud nests in Montana. These belonged to *Maiasaura*. The name means "good mother lizard."

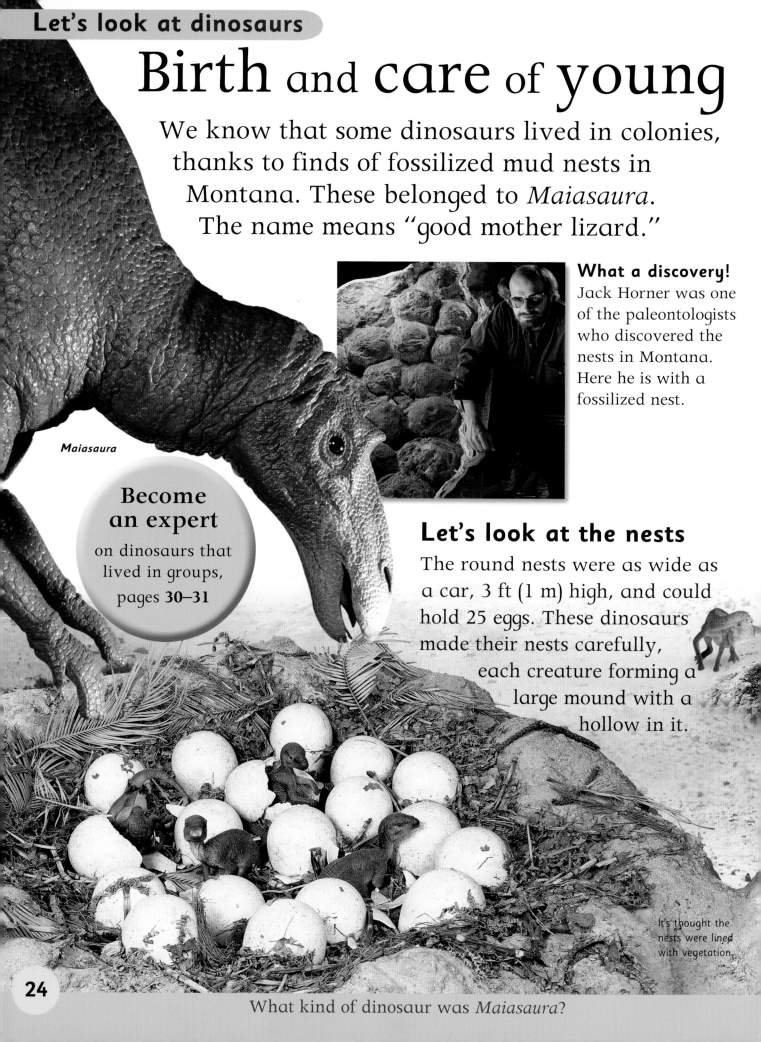

Maiasaura

What a discovery!
Jack Horner was one of the paleontologists who discovered the nests in Montana. Here he is with a fossilized nest.

Become an expert
on dinosaurs that lived in groups, pages **30–31**

Let's look at the nests

The round nests were as wide as a car, 3 ft (1 m) high, and could hold 25 eggs. These dinosaurs made their nests carefully, each creature forming a large mound with a hollow in it.

It's thought the nests were lined with vegetation.

What kind of dinosaur was *Maiasaura*?

Model of *Maiasaura* nest

Some hatchling bones had worn teeth, suggesting they had been fed in the nest or had foraged and returned.

It's safer in the nest!

The nests contained trampled eggshells and some had bones of hatchlings, which suggests the young had remained in the nest after hatching. Similarly, many of today's birds remain in the nest until they can look after themselves.

I'm gonna grow!

The hatched babies weighed about as much as a large phone book and were about 1 ft (30 cm) long. The adult dinosaurs weighed as much as a small car and were as long as a bus.

We're hungry!

Experts don't think there were many plants around the nests, so the mothers probably found food elsewhere and brought it back to their young.

Colony life?

The nests in Montana were spaced out, suggesting they were part of a colony. The spaces acted as pathways between nests and allowed the adults to lie next to the eggs to protect them.

It was a hadrosaur. Learn more about them on pages 70–71.

Hunting

Meat-eaters had to scavenge or hunt to stay alive. Some would have hunted alone, but there is also evidence of pack hunting. This does make it easier to corner and overcome prey. Just think how effective lions are at hunting today.

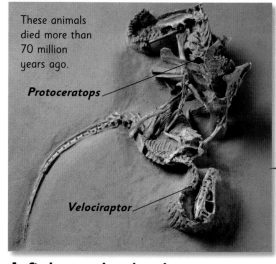

These animals died more than 70 million years ago.

Protoceratops

Velociraptor

A fight to the death

This amazing fossil captured the death throes of a *Protoceratops* and *Velociraptor* locked in combat. It provides proof that *Velociraptor* preyed on *Protoceratops*.

Hunting in packs

Velociraptor may only have been the size of a large dog, but it was probably an incredibly accomplished killer. Its narrow jaws contained bladelike fangs, and its fingers and toes were armed with daggerlike claws.

Velociraptor

Protoceratops

Did dinosaurs ever hunt human beings?

Let's get together

Scientists believe a number of dinosaurs may have hunted in packs, including:

Utahraptor was the largest-known raptor. It prowled western America.

Deinonychus was a 10 ft- (3 m-) long killer that roamed North America.

Giganotosaurus was one of the largest meat-eaters.

A young *Protoceratops* would have had little chance of defending itself against a pack of hungry *Velociraptors*.

Watch out! Rotten teeth!

Some of the large meat-eaters may have delivered a batch of bacteria when they bit. The largest living lizard, the Komodo dragon, has saliva full of bacteria that live on rotting meat stuck in its teeth. Its bite can poison its victim. The same may have applied to some of the dinosaurs.

Komodo dragon

No. Humans appeared about 64 million years after the last dinosaurs.

Go away!

Plant-eating dinosaurs had to find ways to protect themselves against the sharp teeth and claws of meat-eaters. They tended to have tough skin—or armor—and some developed interesting weaponry.

Edmontonia lived at the same time and in the same places as *T. rex*, so it needed tough protection!

Edmontonia

Walking shields

The armored dinosaurs, or ankylosaurs, were fairly tanklike, with their low-to-the-ground appearance and heavily plated backs. There was a huge variety.

Chain mail protection

Stegosaurus is instantly recognizable with its bony plates. It also had bony studs under its neck and on its hips, thighs, and tail. These acted like chain mail in preventing a meat-eater from biting but allowing the *Stegosaurus* to move.

Stegosaurus

Could the ankylosaurs run away from danger?

Swing that club!

Ankylosaurus had a lump of thickened bone at the end of its tail, giving it a club shape. Its muscular tail would swing this club from side to side. It also had thick bone on its head, neck, and body.

Geysers shoot hot water into the air. They are rare today, but may have been more common in the Mesozoic Era.

Ankylosaurus has been described as a "living tank."

Triceratops

Triceratops had a bony shield to protect its neck and shoulders.

Ankylosaurus tail

Tail defense

Tails—especially armored ones—were useful for swinging at predators.

Euoplocephalus had a club made from fused bone at the end of its tail.

Stegosaurus had spikes at the end of its tail that could be over 3 ft (1 m) long.

Diplodocus This sauropod may have used its long tail as a whip.

Stay back!

Triceratops was one of the largest of all horned dinosaurs. It would have been an intimidating dinosaur to try to kill.

Scientists don't think they could run fast, so their body armor was their defense.

It's better with friends

Many of today's animals live in groups, some for protection (antelope) and some for hunting (lions). It is likely that many dinosaurs did the same, and for similar reasons.

Herd of *Iguanodon*

It's noisy here

Just imagine the sounds and clouds of dust as large groups of dinosaurs moved off. Herds of cattle can sound like thunder if they stampede. A herd of hefty dinosaurs must have been a jaw-dropping sight.

Large sauropods may have stuck together in big groups.

This way for food!

If dinosaurs did gather together in large groups, it suggests that some may have been migratory— they moved on in search of fresh grazing much as African wildebeest do today. Large plant-eating sauropods may have trekked massive distances.

How far would dinosaurs have walked in search of fresh grazing?

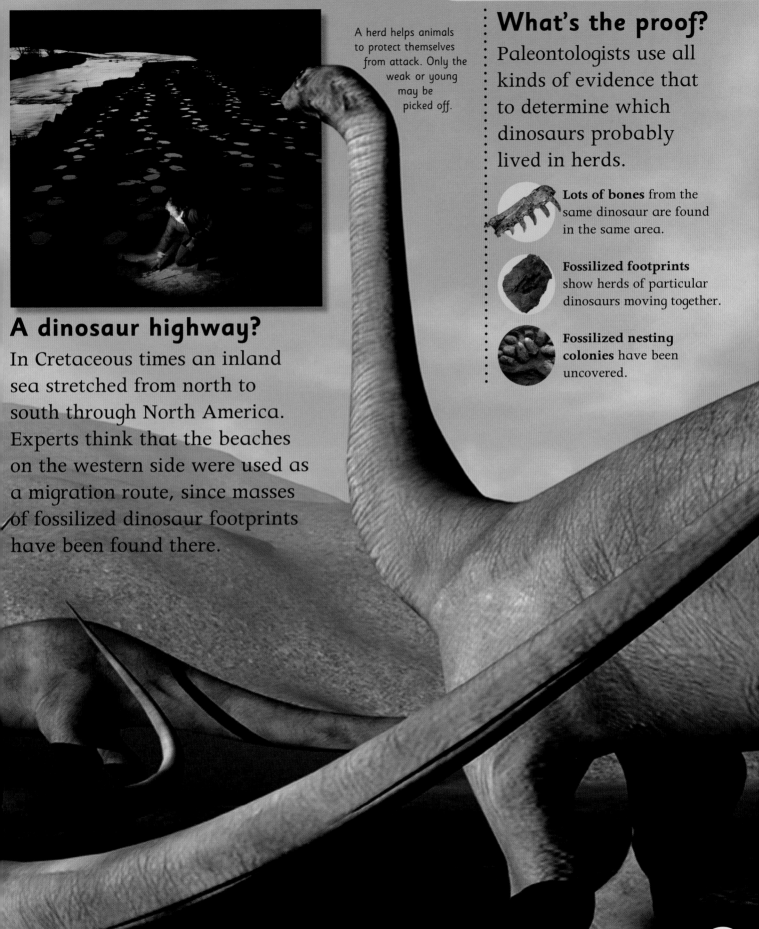

What's the proof?

Paleontologists use all kinds of evidence that to determine which dinosaurs probably lived in herds.

Lots of bones from the same dinosaur are found in the same area.

Fossilized footprints show herds of particular dinosaurs moving together.

Fossilized nesting colonies have been uncovered.

A herd helps animals to protect themselves from attack. Only the weak or young may be picked off.

A dinosaur highway?

In Cretaceous times an inland sea stretched from north to south through North America. Experts think that the beaches on the western side were used as a migration route, since masses of fossilized dinosaur footprints have been found there.

Nobody knows, but wildebeest sometimes migrate 900 miles (1,500 km).

Triassic dinosaurs

Just before the Triassic period Earth suffered a mass extinction (probably caused by climate changes) that wiped out about 96 percent of all living things. It took millions of years before the planet could even begin to recover.

Triassic Earth as it looked between 248 and 206 million years ago.

This is one of the earliest known dinosaurs.

Animal life

Mammal-like reptiles of the early Triassic developed into true mammals by the end of the period.

Eozostrodon, one of the earliest true mammals, fed its young with milk.

Lystrosaurus, an early Triassic mammal-like reptile, was a dog-sized plant-eater.

Megazostrodon, a mammal, was about 5 in (12 cm) long. It may have eaten insects.

Eoraptor

What did the existence of one huge landmass mean for animal life?

So what was Earth like?

In Triassic times, the planet was hot and dry, with huge deserts. There were pockets of fertile land near the coasts, but there were no flowers. Earth would have been unrecognizable to us.

Early dinosaurs would have seen huge areas of hot, red desert.

Herrerasaurus's body shape shows it would have been a fast-moving dinosaur.

Herrerasaurus

Staurikosaurus

New life appears

The Triassic period saw the gradual renewal of life on Earth and the appearance of the largest creatures ever to roam there—dinosaurs.

Curiosity quiz

Look through the Triassic dinosaurs pages to identify the picture clues below.

Become an expert

on *Eoraptor*, pages 42–43
on early mammals, pages 96–97

It meant that land animals were free to roam where they wanted.

The dinosaurs are coming

There were no dinosaurs at the start of the Triassic period. In fact, there was very little life. So where did they come from?

The name archosaur means "ruling lizard."

I was first

The direct ancestors of the dinosaurs were a group of reptiles called the archosaurs.

The largest was the formidable predator *Postosuchus*.

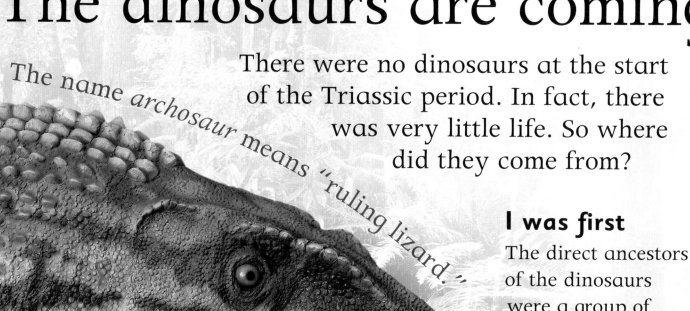

Postosuchus grew to 15 ft (4.5 m) long.

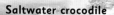
Saltwater crocodile

An ancient history

Today's crocodiles (and birds) are the last surviving archosaurs. Crocodiles have a similar body shape to the Triassic *Desmatosuchus*.

Desmatosuchus

Long shoulder spikes protected the animal's neck.

Was *Desmatosaucus* a crocodile?

Peteinosaurus

Early pterosaurs were not much larger than a modern crow.

Other archosaurs

Postosuchus was not the only archosaur, though it was the most fearsome.

Lagosuchus was just 1 ft (30 cm) in length.

Euparkeria was slightly larger, at 2 ft (60 cm) in length.

Chasmatosaurus reached lengths of 6 ft 6 in (2 m).

We were there!
Pterosaurs were flying reptiles, not dinosaurs, and they appeared in late Triassic skies. One of the first pterosaurs was *Peteinosaurus*.

Eudimorphodon

We are dinosaurs!
Some of the most primitive dinosaurs belong to a group called the coelurosaurs, a name that means "hollow-tailed reptile."

Coelophysis were just 6–10 ft (2–3 m) in length.

Bony plates covered *Desmatosuchus's* back and tail, and part of its belly.

weird or what?
Although the mighty *T. rex* did not appear for another 160 million years, it is descended from the coelurosaurs.

No, but it was closely related.

Petrified Forest

The Petrified Forest in Arizona
is packed with late Triassic
fossils of plants and animals.

Placerias

I'm not a dinosaur
The fossils in Arizona
give us some idea of
the kinds of animals
that the first dinosaurs
would have met.
Placerias was
a large reptile,
growing up to
9 ft (2.7 m) long.

The trees were huge,
originally standing
at about 200 ft (60 m)
in height.

Floodwaters covered
the bases of the trees,
uprooting many.

Is that a crocodile?
Phytosaurs were crocodilelike reptiles.
Some species grew as long as buses—
up to 40 ft (12 m).

What dinosaur fossils have been found in the Petrified Forest?

Remains of a forest

Ancient fossilized trees dot the ground in the
Petrified Forest. They are all that remain of
a once mighty Triassic forest of conifer trees.
So how have the trees been preserved
for 220 million years?

*Chindesaurus
had particularly
long hind legs.*

Chindesaurus

An early dinosaur
Chindesaurus is one
of North America's
earliest-known
dinosaurs. It could
probably move
fast when hunting.

Over millions of years,
the trees were buried in
gravelly sand. Gradually,
they turned to stone.

Millions of years
later the land
eroded, exposing
the fossilized trunks.

37

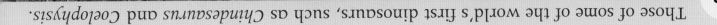

Triassic plant-eaters

The Triassic saw the emergence of the prosauropods, an early type of sauropod (a dinosaur group that appeared later).

A long-named prosauropod
Thecodontosaurus was the first Triassic prosauropod to be named. It was a very primitive plant-eating dinosaur with saw-edged teeth.

The first large dinosaur

Plateosaurus is believed to have been the first large dinosaur, reaching about 26 ft (8 m) in length. Scientists believe that it was one of the most common of late Triassic dinosaurs.

Like most prosauropods, *Plateosaurus* was a plant-eater.

Become an expert
on sauropods, pages 52–55

Where have *Plateosaurus* fossils been found?

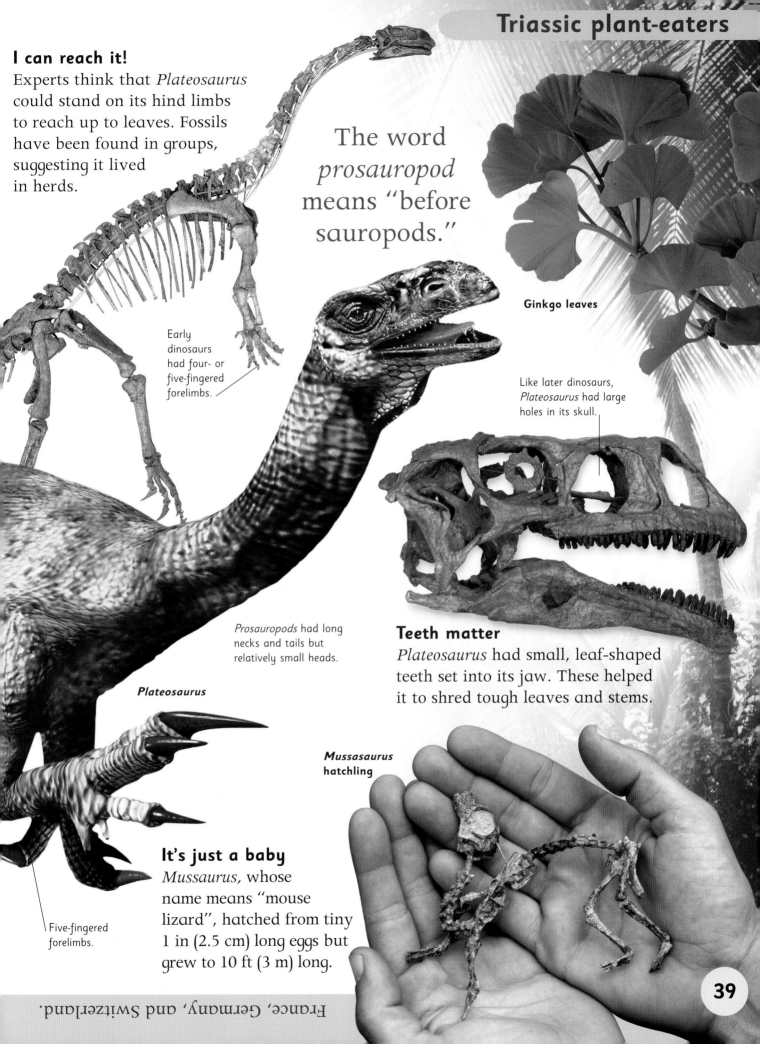

I can reach it!

Experts think that *Plateosaurus* could stand on its hind limbs to reach up to leaves. Fossils have been found in groups, suggesting it lived in herds.

The word *prosauropod* means "before sauropods."

Ginkgo leaves

Early dinosaurs had four- or five-fingered forelimbs.

Like later dinosaurs, *Plateosaurus* had large holes in its skull.

Prosauropods had long necks and tails but relatively small heads.

Plateosaurus

Teeth matter

Plateosaurus had small, leaf-shaped teeth set into its jaw. These helped it to shred tough leaves and stems.

Mussasaurus hatchling

Five-fingered forelimbs.

It's just a baby

Mussaurus, whose name means "mouse lizard", hatched from tiny 1 in (2.5 cm) long eggs but grew to 10 ft (3 m) long.

France, Germany, and Switzerland.

From small beginnings

Early plant-eaters were small, but by the end of the Triassic, some grew to huge proportions.

Melanorosaurus

Riojasaurus

Melanorosaurus, or "black mountain lizard," was a bulky, four-footed plant-eater and possibly one of the first sauropods.

Lesothosaurus   Pisanosaurus

Mussasaurus hatchling   Adult human

Don't get in the way!

Riojasaurus was a heavily built herbivore that grew to about 30–36 feet (9–11 m) in length. It had a long neck, body, and tail.

Riojasaurus

Dog-sized
Pisanosaurus was small, and the earliest known plant-eating dinosaur. It probably fed on low-growing plants.

Pisanosaurus

Do you think a *Riojasaurus* could run?

It's so tiny!

Remember *Mussaurus*, which we met on page 39? Here is another picture of this baby dinosaur's skull. Large dinosaurs started off small, but they grew and grew and grew. *Mussaurus* is the smallest fossilized dinosaur skeleton known.

When fully grown, a *Mussaurus* would have weighed about 260 lbs (120 kg).

Become an expert

on what Triassic dinosaurs would have seen and eaten, pages 10–11

Riojasaurus had spoon-shaped, serrated teeth.

Teeth talk

Riojasaurus would have used its teeth to pull needles and twigs from conifer trees. It may have swallowed them whole to be ground up in its stomach.

Plodding along

Riojasaurus moved slowly on thick, elephantlike legs. It probably lived in large herds for protection from predators.

Lesothosaurus

This small dinosaur appeared as the Triassic slipped into the Jurassic, making it one of the last Triassic dinosaurs.

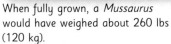

Lesothosaurus

It would have been unable to run very fast.

We're looking for meat!

As with today's animals, there were more plant-eaters than meat-eaters in the world of the dinosaurs. One of the earliest meat-eaters was the *Eoraptor*.

Scientists believe *Eoraptor* lived 228 million years ago.

Old dinosaur bones

Just 3 ft (1 m) long, the fierce *Eoraptor* was only recently discovered and named when a near-complete skeleton was found in Argentina, South America, in 1991. The skeleton had been beautifully fossilized.

Eoraptor was probably a fast runner.

Hands and feet had sharp claws.

What does the name *Eoraptor* mean?

Staurikosaurus

This small meat-eater, or theropod, is another early dinosaur. It was a little bigger than *Eoraptor*, but still slender, and probably only the weight of a nine-year-old child.

Lightly built body

Long, thin tail used for balance.

Four-fingered hands

Adult human

Eoraptor

Eoraptor   *Staurikosaurus*

Eoraptor

Staurikosaurus

We're ready to bite

Eoraptor probably ate lizards and small mammal-like reptiles, efficiently tearing into them with its sharp, curved front teeth.

Eoraptor had large eyes, so probably enjoyed good vision.

Dinosaur claws

As dinosaurs evolved, it seems that the number of fingers on their forelimbs decreased.

Like many early dinosaurs, *Eoraptor* had five-fingered hands.

Four or five fingers were found on early dinosaurs, such as *Thecodontosaurus*.

Three fingers were found on later dinosaurs, such as *Allosaurus*.

Two fingers were found on many Cretaceous dinosaurs, such as *T. rex*.

Become an expert

on pack hunters, pages 26–27

"Dawn thief."

Herrera's dinosaur

Find an unknown dinosaur and it may be named after you. That's what happened to Victorino Herrera after he found fragments of a dinosaur fossil in 1958.

Victorino Herrera's dinosaur was named *Herrerasaurus.* It was one of the earliest dinosaurs.

The slender legs were well-muscled.

Herrerasaurus

weird or what?

Triassic days were shorter than our days. That's because the Earth spun a little faster in Triassic times. It meant that a Triassic day lasted 22¾ hours rather than 24!

The longest three fingers had curved claws.

Where did Victorino Herrera find the fragments of *Herrerasaurus*?

What did it eat?

Herrerasaurus probably ate mammal-like reptiles called cynodonts, like these:

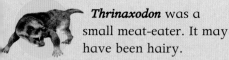

Thrinaxodon was a small meat-eater. It may have been hairy.

Cynognathus was a ferocious predator with long, doglike teeth.

Diademodon was a plant-eater that grew to the size of a small cow.

Pisanosaurus

Looking out for something small

As well as cynodonts *Herrerasaurus* may have feasted on smaller dinosaurs, such as *Pisanosaurus*. Its light frame would have helped it to be a stealthy hunter.

Head talk

Herrerasaurus had a long pointed head and sharp, saw-edged teeth. Its jaw was double-hinged to help it grip its prey.

The jaws were well-designed to grip struggling prey.

A long tail helped to balance the body.

A rare find

A near-complete skeleton of *Herrerasaurus* was found in 1988 near the Andes Mountains, South America. It showed the dinosaur to be one of the largest hunters of its time. It was a little longer than a car.

Herrerasaurus

Pisanosaurus

In Argentina, where he lived.

Edwin Colbert (left) with members of his team.

Ghost Ranch

A fossil quarry in New Mexico is the site of one of the most incredible dinosaur finds ever. Hundreds of dinosaurs died there.

What was found?

In 1947, Edwin H. Colbert documented the discovery of hundreds of well-preserved *Coelophysis* skeletons. This meat-eating dinosaur was one of Earth's first dinosaurs.

Herd of *Coelophysis*

A look at *Coelophysis*
Coelophysis was about 8 ft (2.4 m) long and weighed about 50 pounds (23 kg). Its long, slender jaws were lined with sharp teeth— evidence that it ate meat.

How did Ghost Ranch get its name?

Ghost Ranch today

Ghost Ranch is a barren place today, but 220 million years ago it was crisscrossed with rivers prone to flooding.

At Ghost Ranch, *Coelophysis* fossils were discovered under just 2 ft (60 cm) of rock.

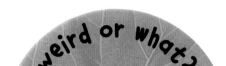

weird or what?

Some people believe there were hangings at Ghost Ranch, and its desert lands are haunted by the dead.

Fossilized *Coelophysis* skeletons

Locked in death

The fossilized skeletons were twisted around each other and paleontologists believe that they all died together, their deaths caused by flash floods.

Groups of skeletons were found together.

Large eye sockets suggest *Coelophysis* had keen eyesight.

Were they cannibals?

One *Coelophysis* fossil has a young *Coelophysis* skeleton among its ribs, suggesting that adults preyed on younger and weaker members of their own kind. Many modern-day reptiles do the same.

Coelophysis probably walked on its hind limbs and used its forelimbs to catch and hold prey.

The young skeleton can be seen in the animal's stomach area.

The fossil quarry is named after a nearby farm.

Jurassic dinosaurs

During the Jurassic the supercontinent Pangaea began to break apart. The oceans spread over what had been land and huge areas flooded. The result was widespread shallow seas and milder weather.

Jurassic Earth as it looked between 206 and 144 million years ago.

Brachiosaurus

Dryosaurus

Sauropods may occasionally have walked through water, but they did not live in water.

So what was Earth like?

Gradually Earth's habitats became less extreme, encouraging more plant variety and the gradual growth of rain forests. There were fewer areas of desert. Dinosaurs moved to new lands, some roaming huge distances.

Did *T. rex* live during the Jurassic period?

Animal life

The Jurassic saw the appearance of giant plant-eating sauropods, such as *Brachiosaurus*, *Seismosaurus*, and *Diplodocus*. Large meat-eaters also emerged, with killers such as *Allosaurus* and *Dilophosaurus* ready to eat anything they could catch. The dinosaurs ruled the Earth.

Seismosaurus

Diplodocus

Allosaurus

Curiosity quiz
Look through the Jurassic dinosaurs pages to identify each of the picture clues below.

Become an expert
on sauropods, pages 50–51
on *Allosaurus*, pages 58–59

No, it came later, during the Cretaceous period.

Sauropods

Sauropods were the heaviest, longest, and tallest animals ever to walk on land. They were herbivores and would have had to graze continually.

Tiny-brained eating machines

Diplodocus skull

Sauropods had tiny heads compared to their bodies. Peg-shaped teeth were used to pull up vegetation.

Peg-shaped teeth.

Around the world

Sauropods have been found all over the world.

Mamenchisaurus grew to 72 ft (22 m) in length in Jurassic China.

Camarasaurus reached a montrous 75 ft (23 m) in Jurassic North America.

Barapasaurus grew to lengths of 59 ft (18 m) and roamed Jurassic India.

Vulcanodon was just 21 ft (6.5 m) when it prowled Jurassic Zimbabwe.

Look at the size of it!

Imagine a dinosaur that was as long as a tennis court—an adult *Diplodocus* was!

Diplodocus's neck and tail made up most of its length.

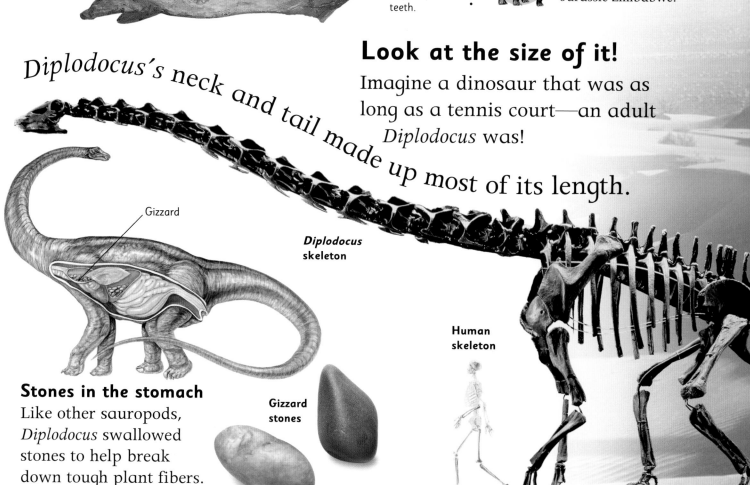

Gizzard

Diplodocus skeleton

Stones in the stomach

Like other sauropods, *Diplodocus* swallowed stones to help break down tough plant fibers.

Gizzard stones

Human skeleton

How many neck vertebrae does the *Diplodocus* have?

It's like a giraffe!

Brachiosaurus had longer forelimbs than hind limbs so its back sloped down to its hindquarters—rather like a giraffe. But *Brachiosaurus* could reach two or three times higher than a giraffe.

Up high
Brachiosaurus nibbled leaves at the tops of trees. Its long neck may have developed so *Brachiosaurus* could feed where other plant-eaters could not reach.

Join hands with eight friends and stretch out your arms. That's about the length of *Brachiosaurus's* neck!

Sauropods had long tails that helped to balance their bodies.

Sauropods under attack

A sauropod's size was its defense—
a fully grown, healthy adult would
have been too large to attack. Some
were massive. However, the young and
sick were vulnerable.

The height of defense

A *Barosaurus* may have
reared up to protect its
young. Standing on its
hind legs, it would have
been as tall as a four-story
building—about 50 ft (15 m).

Replica neck bones of a
Barosaurus are carried
to an exhibition in
New York City.

Barosaurus

How long could a sauropod live?

Seismosaurus

Barosaurus   Apatosaurus   Human

Seismosaurus was 110 ft (34 m) long.

Seismosaurus means "earth-shaking lizard." The ground certainly would have shaken as it walked along.

A whip in the tail
A tail can make a good whip, and scientists believe that *Apatosaurus* (originally called *Brontosaurus*) may have whipped its tail at predators. This could have resulted in a nasty injury.

On the attack
There was no shortage of Jurassic meat-eating dinosaurs.

Ceratosaurus lived on tree-covered plains and ate dinosaurs and reptiles.

Saurophaganax is thought by scientists to be a type of *Allosaurus*.

Torvosaurus had a bulky body and was the largest carnivore of its time.

Look up!
Seismosaurus is the longest dinosaur ever found. It weighed as much as six elephants.

Allosaurus bit into its prey, then pulled its head up, tearing away flesh.

weird or what?
Seismosaurus eggs have been found in lines, not in nests. Scientists believe the animals may have laid their eggs while they walked along!

Cetiosaurus

Meet an ancient giant—the *Cetiosaurus*. On a diet of ferns and trees it grew to huge proportions. Its thigh bone alone was 6 ft (1.8 m) in length. That's the height of a fully grown man!

We are family!

Like all dinosaurs, *Cetiosaurus* belongs to a family. It is a cetiosauridae and members are found all over the world. Here's one of its Chinese cousins, *Shunosaurus*.

Shunosaurus

It's not a whale!

The first sauropod to be found, and one of the first dinosaurs to be named, *Cetiosaurus* was believed to be related to the whale because its backbones, or vertebrae, were similar to those of a whale.

Cetiosaurus vertebra

Whale vertebrae

So just how big?

Although only medium-sized for a sauropod, *Cetiosaurus* grew to an impressive 53 ft (16 m) in length. Large herds lived along the shore of an ancient sea in England.

What does the name *Cetiosaurus* mean?

What about elsewhere?

The huge *Rhoetosaurus* was one of Australia's largest Jurassic dinosaurs. Its great weight meant it probably walked slowly and did not run.

Large feet spread *Rhoetosaurus's* weight over a wide area.

Hungry predators

A number of hungry Jurassic meat-eaters might have killed and eaten *Cetiosaurus.*

Megalosaurus was 26 ft (8 m) long. It had curved teeth and long, sharp claws.

Eustreptospondylus was a 16–22 ft- (5–6.5 m-) tall, lightly built hunter.

Allosaurus was 39 ft (12 m) long with knifelike teeth that sliced into its prey.

Become an expert on living in herds, pages 30–31

"Whalelike lizard."

We ate plants, too!

The bulky sauropods weren't the only herbivorous dinosaurs in the Jurassic world. A variety of small, plant-eating dinosaurs were also competing for food.

Tough stalks? No problem!
Unlike the sauropods, many smaller plant-eaters had horny, toothless beaks and ridged cheek teeth. These were perfect for stripping tough leaves from woody stems.

Other herbivores
Here are some more Jurassic plant-eaters that you may not know.

Heterodontosaurus, the "different-toothed lizard," had three kinds of teeth.

Lufengosaurus had a horse-sized body. It was a sturdily built prosauropod.

Lesothosaurus had a slim body that was only the size of a small goat.

Were two legs best?
These plant-eaters may have been small, but their ability to walk on two legs made them unusually agile.

How do we know so much about the plants the dinosaurs ate?

Camptosaurus

Camptosaurus skeleton

I'm a survivor
This dinosaur spans two periods: it survived from the late Triassic into the early Cretaceous in North America and England.

Cycads resembled palms we see today, but they didn't produce flowers.

Scutellosaurus

The bony spikes would have made *Scutellosaurus* a lot heavier than other similar-sized dinosaurs.

Don't eat me!
In addition to good agility, some plant-eaters had extra protection. *Scutellosaurus* was covered with more than 300 little bony spikes on its back, sides, and tail.

Conifer trees were plentiful long before the dinosaurs came along.

Horsetails grew taller than many trees in the Mezozoic Era.

Dryosaurus

Ferns were around long before the appearance of the dinosaurs.

Parrot face
Dryosaurus had a parrotlike beak, which it used to crop plants that it then crushed up with its leaf-shaped teeth. It probably lived in herds in East Africa and North America.

Dryosaurus was perfectly built to run away from danger—fast!

Become an expert
on what dinosaurs saw, pages 10–11

57

We know because there are lots of fossilized plants.

Killers on the loose

Huge and powerful meat-eaters roamed during the Jurassic. Scientists aren't sure if they hunted singly or in packs, but they would have been formidable predators even when hunting alone.

Become an expert

on Triassic meat-eaters, pages 42–45

on a Cretaceous meat-eater, pages 76–77

Allosaurus

This meat-eater used its good hearing and sense of smell to find a victim. It may have hidden in bushes and jumped out on prey that walked by.

Where was the first almost-complete *Allosaurus* found?

What an odd head

Dilophosaurus, a large two-legged predator, had a semicircular bony crest on each side of its skull. These may have helped cool the dinosaur or been used as part of a mating display.

Bony crest

Dilophosaurus prowled long before *Allosaurus* came on the scene.

Dilophosaurus

What a big head

Allosaurus's head was 3 ft (1 m) long. Special joints allowed the animal to open its jaws extra wide, exposing about 70 teeth, some 4 in (10 cm) long.

A savage hand

Allosaurus's muscled forearms ended in three-digit, grasping hands. They were equipped with savage, hooked claws.

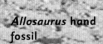

Allosaurus hand fossil

Colorado.

China's killers

Yangchuanosaurus is hunting. This large meat-eater has spotted a weak *Mamenchisaurus*, a supersized plant-eater, and is waiting for its chance to attack.

What's that dinosaur?

Yangchuanosaurus was a large meat-eater that hunted in Jurassic China. With a head the size of an armchair, it would have been a frightening sight.

Deadly dinosaurs

During the Jurassic, dinosaur numbers continued to grow. Here are more meat-eaters from China.

Dilophosaurus, from the early Jurassic, was found in China and the US.

Monolophosaurus, one of the first giant meat-eaters, was from the mid-Jurassic.

Szechuanosaurus, from the late Jurassic, looked like a small *Allosaurus*.

As with all dinosaurs, we can only guess at this one's skin color and patterning.

Yangchuanosaurus

Mamenchisaurus's long tail helped to balance its neck (in the same way as a seesaw).

What did *Mamenchisaurus* eat?

There's the end
Mamenchisaurus's long neck was supported by 19 vertebrae. That's the highest number of neck bones of any known dinosaur. The bones were hollow; otherwise the neck would have been too heavy to lift.

Mamenchisaurus's head was less than 2 ft (61 cm) long.

Mamenchisaurus

Famed for its neck
Mamenchisaurus had an absurdly long neck. In fact, its neck was more than half the length of the whole animal and it is currently known as the longest necked animal ever. Its head, in comparison, was tiny.

It's doubtful that Mamenchisaurus could bend its neck very much.

weird or what?
The Moon was a little closer to Earth in Triassic and Jurassic times, making it appear larger in the sky. It would have reflected more of the Sun's light, and so have appeared brighter.

61

Plants, including conifers, seed ferns, club mosses, and horsetails.

Little and large

Although they would not have met, *Compsognathus* and *Ceratosaurus* both lived during the Jurassic—one on warm islands and one on floodplains.

Tiny bones were found in the stomach area.

Fossilized *Compsognathus*

Fossil evidence

Compsognathus was found in 1861, but not at first recognized as a dinosaur since it was thought to be too small. One fossil was found with its last meal inside it—a lizard.

Compsognathus was named for its jaw. The name means "pretty jaw."

Compsognathus was about the size of a chicken.

Compsognathus

Compsognathus lived on a group of islands where Europe is now. It was a fierce (though small) predator.

What did *Compsognathus* eat?

Ceratosaurus

Ceratosaurus was 15–20 ft (4.5–6 m) long. It was a powerful meat-eating dinosaur with a short horn on its head.

Ceratosaurs

Ceratosaurus belongs to a family of dinosaurs called ceratosaurs. Other members include:

Dilophosaurus had two almost semicircular crests on its head.

Coelophysis was about 6 ft (1.8 m) long and looked like a long-legged bird.

Segisaurus was a small ceratosaur, at just 3 ft (1 m) long.

Ceratosaurus had bony knobs and ridges on its head, spine, and at the end of its tail.

Flexible tail

Ceratosaurus means "horned lizard."

Become an expert
on fossils,
pages **100–101**

Ceratosaurus

Human

Compsognathus

This dinosaur had a fourth toe.

A national monument

From 1909 to 1924, scientists removed 330 tons (300 metric tons) of late Jurassic dinosaur bones from a quarry in Utah. The importance of the find was recognized by the creation of the Dinosaur National Monument there in 1915.

Bones in the wall

The Dinosaur National Monument has a visitor's center built around a wall that contains more than 1,500 dinosaur fossils.

A different landscape

In dinosaur times, the area in Utah where the dinosaurs were found was a watering hole. That's why so many creatures gathered there.

How long do you think it took Earl Douglass to remove the *Apatosaurus* skeleton he found?

Plant-eaters

Three-quarters of the bones found at the monument belong to sauropods, such as *Apatosaurus*, *Camarasaurus*, and *Diplodocus*.

Apatosaurus lived about 150 million years ago.

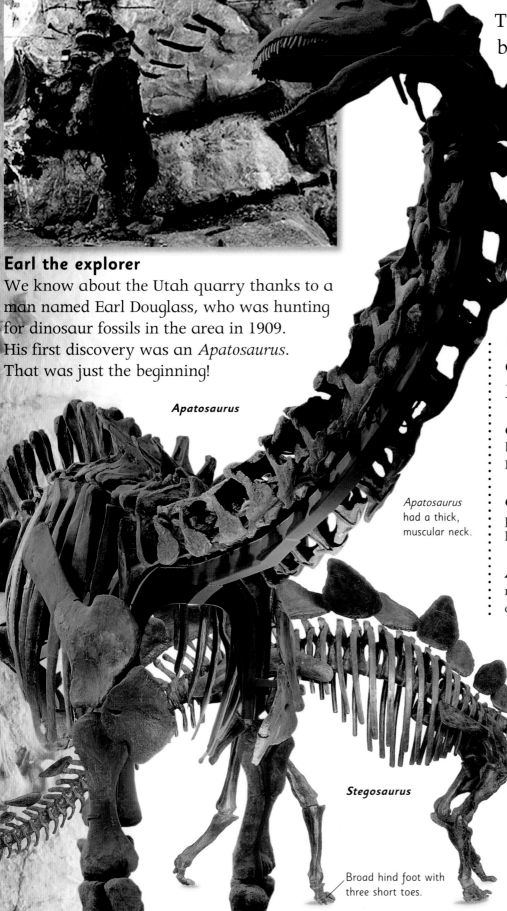

Earl the explorer

We know about the Utah quarry thanks to a man named Earl Douglass, who was hunting for dinosaur fossils in the area in 1909. His first discovery was an *Apatosaurus*. That was just the beginning!

Apatosaurus

Apatosaurus had a thick, muscular neck.

Meat-eaters

Three types of meat-eaters have been found at Dinosaur National Monument.

Ceratosaurus had a bony horn on its nose. It was a big dinosaur.

Ornitholestes probably preyed on small lizards.

Allosaurus was a large meat-eater. Learn more on page 59.

The bony plates would have made this dinosaur appear much bigger than it actually was.

I recognize that one!

A complete *Stegosaurus* skeleton was found at the monument. This was a small-headed plant-eater that has become famous for its bony plates.

Stegosaurus

Broad hind foot with three short toes.

65

Cretaceous dinosaurs

At this time, Earth's continents had separated and were beginning to drift apart. On each one, dinosaurs developed in different ways, so the number of different types of dinosaur increased significantly.

Cretaceous Earth as it looked between 144 and 65 million years ago.

So what was Earth like?

The beginning of the Cretaceous period saw similar temperatures to those in the Jurassic, but over the next million years or so, temperatures began to cool. The Earth we know was beginning to emerge.

Corythosaurus

Triceratops

What plants appeared in the Cretaceous that hadn't been present before?

Animal life

The Cretaceous period saw a huge variety of dinosaurs, from plant-eaters such as *Iguanodon* and *Triceratops* to meat-eaters such as *Troodon* and *T. rex*. This was the last time the dinosaurs would inhabit Earth, and they flourished.

T. rex

Troodon

Curiosity quiz

Look through the Cretaceous dinosaurs pages to identify each of the picture clues below.

Become an expert

on *Troodon*, pages 82–83
on horned dinosaurs, pages 72–73

Flowering plants (you can learn more on page 11).

67

Dinosaur Provincial Park

Today, Dinosaur Provincial Park in Alberta, Canada, is rocky and fairly bare. Seventy-five million years ago, it was a subtropical paradise, based around the marshy mouth of a river. It was also the site of an incredible amount of dinosaur activity.

Dinosaur Provincial Park has proved a treasure trove for dinosaur fossils since the first find in 1910.

Fossilized *Corythosaurus* skeleton

Fabulous fossilization

Many of the Park's dinosaur skeletons have been well-preserved because of the original marshy ground; just look at this *Corythosaurus,* a hadrosaur.

Corythosaurus

What's been found?

Thirty-five species of late Cretaceous dinosaurs have been found at the Park, and a total of 300 skeletons removed. Most common were the hadrosaurs.

It's a tank!
Euoplocephalus, a plant-eater, was well protected from a possible attack.

What was a key feature of ankylosaurs?

Turtle fossil

What else was found?
In addition to dinosaurs, scientists have found the fossilized skeletons of many other Cretaceous creatures at the Park. These include lots of fish, crocodiles, pterosaurs, birds, mammals, and turtles.

Will he eat me?
Albertosaurus was the Park's largest predator. It would have had plenty of hadrosaurs to feed on.

Armored tanks
Three kinds of ankylosaur dinosaurs have been found at Provincial Park.

Panoplosaurus had long shoulder spikes, as well as bony plates on its back.

Edmontonia was covered with rows of bony plates and spikes.

Euoplocephalus used a hefty lump of bone on its tail for protection.

Albertosaurus looked a little bit like *T. rex*. In fact, it was related to *T. rex*, but it appeared first.

Is that a bony head?
Pachycephalosaurus had an incredibly thick bone on its skull. Can you think why? Find out more about this dinosaur on page 20.

Euoplocephalus

More than 170 different types of plants grew in the area.

Pachycephalosaurus

Become an expert
on ankylosaurs, pages 74–75
on hadrosaurs, pages 70–71

Most ankylosaurs were heavily armored.

Cretaceous cows

All kinds of crests

Those striking crests came in all kinds of different shapes.

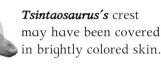

Corythosaurus had a platelike crest.

Tsintaosaurus's crest may have been covered in brightly colored skin.

Lambeosaurus had a helmetlike crest.

Hadrosaurs were basically the cows of the Cretaceous. They would have been a familiar sight in the forests and swamps of North America.

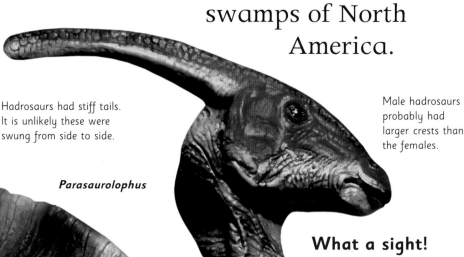

Hadrosaurs had stiff tails. It is unlikely these were swung from side to side.

Parasaurolophus

Male hadrosaurs probably had larger crests than the females.

What a sight!

Hadrosaurs are known for having some of the strangest heads of all dinosaurs; many of them had a crest.

Become an expert

on another hadrosaur, *Maiasaura*, pages **24–25**

Can you think of any crested animals today?

A hadrosaur had more than 1,000 teeth (though not all were in use at the same time!).

Did they have beaks?

That ducklike beak contained tightly packed rows of teeth to grind the vegetation.

Fossilized hadrosaur teeth

Chew and move on

A hadrosaur such as *Corythosaurus* would have roamed in huge herds, grazing on leaves, pine needles, and ferns.

What did they eat?

One hadrosaur fossil contained the remains of its last meal: pine cones, conifer needles, bark, and branches. This tough plant matter is particularly hard to digest!

Corythosaurus

71

A number of lizards and birds have crests.

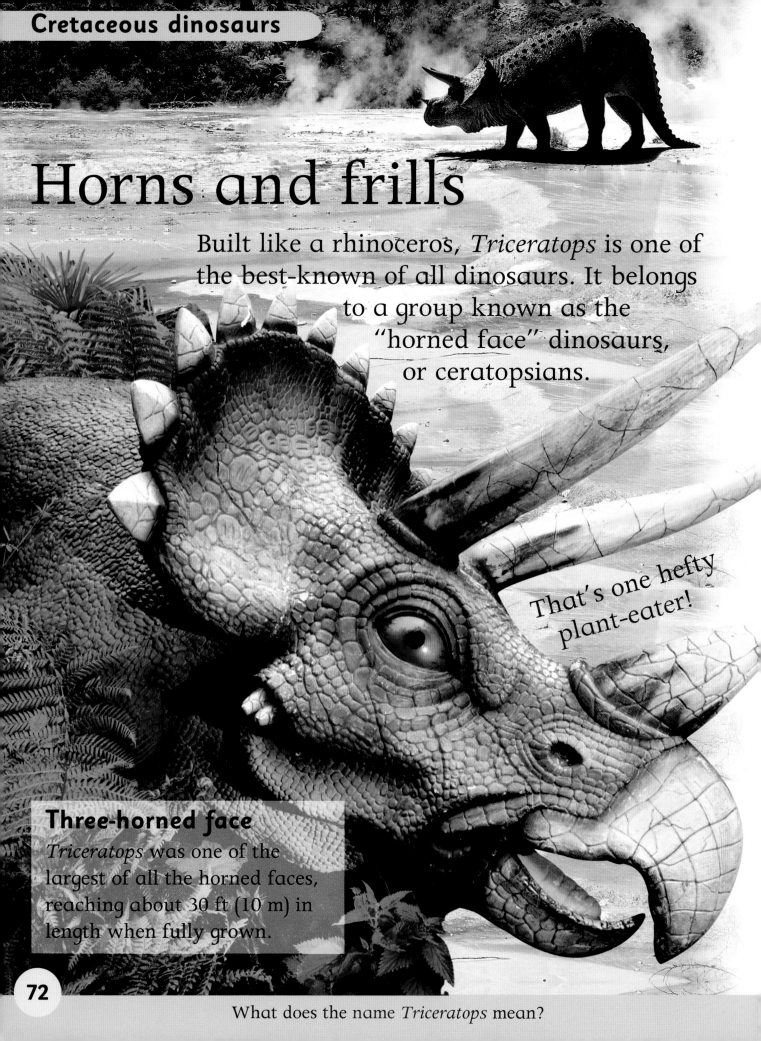

Horns and frills

Built like a rhinoceros, *Triceratops* is one of the best-known of all dinosaurs. It belongs to a group known as the "horned face" dinosaurs, or ceratopsians.

That's one hefty plant-eater!

Three-horned face

Triceratops was one of the largest of all the horned faces, reaching about 30 ft (10 m) in length when fully grown.

What does the name *Triceratops* mean?

Other ceratopsians

There were a number of different dinosaurs with horns and frills:

Protoceratops, which had a head frill but lacked a horn.

Styracosaurus, or "spiked lizard," had a fancy, horned frill.

Pentaceratops had an enormous neck frill and three long horns.

Sheep of the Gobi

Protoceratops roamed the Gobi Desert in Asia rather as sheep roam today. In fact, they were about the size of sheep.

Like all the horn-face dinosaurs, *Protoceratops* had a parrotlike beak.

From baby Protoceratops to fully grown adult.

Fully developed skull

Hatchling

Not a fighter

Protoceratops lacked any protection. Its small size would have made it the ideal prey for a number of meat-eaters.

One big dinosaur graveyard

The Gobi Desert is littered with the remains of *Protoceratops*, and they show all stages of growth.

73

"Three-horned face."

Ankylosaurus
skull

Armored tanks

The ankylosaurs were the armored tanks of the dinosaur world. These four-legged dinosaurs had their own form of protection, since they were covered in thick bony plates and spikes.

Armored head

Ankylosaurs were protected from head to tail. Just look at the solid appearance of these fossilized skulls.

Euoplocephalus
skull

Armored giant

At one time, *Euoplocephalus* was a common ankylosaur on the plains of North America. This creature was well protected from predators, as it had fused bony plates over its neck and back.

Euoplocephalus

Spikes and studs added extra protection along its back.

Broad beak for cropping ferns and low-growing plants.

Were ankylosaurs meat-eaters or plant-eaters?

Ankylosaurs

Ankylosaurs can be separated into groups depending on their appearance. There are three main groups:

Ankylosaurids, such as *Ankylosaurus*, had bony clubs on their tails.

Nodosaurids, such as *Edmontonia*, had rows of spikes on their bodies.

Polacanthids, such as *Gastonia*, had spiked bodies and tails.

Impressions in rock show that *Saltasaurus* had bony studs.

Saltasaurus

Armored sauropods, too!

The ankylosaurs were not the only Cretaceous dinosaurs to have armor. Some sauropods did, too. Just look at this studded *Saltasaurus*.

Ankylosaurus tail club

Clubbed tail

Some ankylosaurs had a tail club made of fused bone that they would swing at attackers. The weighty club would have been a formidable weapon.

They were plant-eaters.

T. rex

T. rex's eyeballs were the size of a clenched fist.

The mighty *T. rex* roamed North America in the last couple of million years that dinosaurs ruled the planet.

Titanic teeth

T. rex had awesome, curved teeth, each as long as a human hand. Altogether it had 58 of these pointed weapons.

Hunter or scavenger?

T. rex preyed on plant-eaters such as *Triceratops*.

T. rex walked on its powerful hind limbs.

When teeth broke, new ones grew to replace them.

Was it a killer?

We don't really know if *T. rex* was a hunter or a scavenger. It may have attacked and killed or it may have picked at dead or dying dinosaurs. It may have done both.

T. rex is short for *Tyrannosaurus rex*. What does it mean?

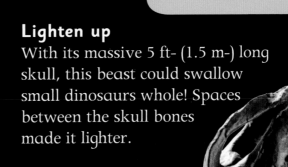

Lighten up

With its massive 5 ft- (1.5 m-) long skull, this beast could swallow small dinosaurs whole! Spaces between the skull bones made it lighter.

A *T. rex* had tiny serrations on its teeth. Its bite would have torn into a victim's flesh.

Guanlong was just 3 ft 8 in (1.1 m) tall, but most of that was tail and neck!

My ancestor

One of the oldest members of the tyrannosaur family was recently found in China. *Guanlong* prowled Earth some 100 million years before *T. rex*.

What a whopper!

Meet Sue, the world's largest and most complete *T. rex* skeleton. She was sold to an American museum in 1991 for a jaw-dropping $8 million.

Nose to tail, Sue measures 42 ft (12.8 m).

Tyrannosaurus rex means "king of the tyrant lizards."

Big and bold

Giganotosaurus means "giant southern reptile," and this dinosaur was big; in fact, it was even larger than *T. rex*. However, the two never met since *Giganotosaurus* was roaming some 10 million years before *T. rex*!

It's a new find!
Giganotosaurus bones were first unearthed in Argentina in the early 1990s, but no complete skeleton has ever been found.

Giganotosaurus would have had a keen sense of smell and excellent eyesight.

weird or what?

It's difficult to imagine just how big and heavy a fully grown *Giganotosaurus* really was. It's thought to have been as heavy as about 125 adult humans. That's a lot of people!

Where did *Giganotosaurus* live?

Let's get it!

A huge sauropod, *Argentinosaurus*, lived alongside *Giganotosaurus*. It's thought that this monster may have reached 140 ft (43 m) in length. So one 45 ft- (14 m-) long *Giganotosaurus* couldn't have brought it down, but these predators may have hunted in packs.

Argentinosaurus

Become an expert

on sauropods, pages 50–55
on *T. rex,* pages 76–77

Awesome arms

Giganotosaurus had larger and more powerful forearms than *T. rex*, and they were three-fingered. It would have used them to grasp prey and food.

That's some tooth!

Gigantosaurus had large, serrated teeth for stabbing and gripping prety, and then for slashing through the meat. The largest teeth were about 8 in (20 cm) in length.

In the warm swamps of Cretaceous Argentina.

Spinosaurus

If there is a contender for the dinosaur that most resembled a dragon, then surely this is it. With its tall "sail" and long, narrow jaws, *Spinosaurus* would have been a frightening sight.

What's that on its back?

Spinosaurus had an impressive skin "sail" that ran the length of its back. It was supported by a number of 6 ft- (2 m-) long bones.

African elephant

What was it for?

The sail bones were covered with a fine mesh of tiny veins, just like an elephant's ears. Just like an elephant cools itself by flapping its ears, the sail may have helped to cool the *Spinosaurus*.

Was *Spinosaurus* bigger than *T. rex*?

Did it look like that?

No one actually knows what color any particular dinosaur was. *Spinosaurus* could have been a dull shade, or it may have been more brightly decorated.

Spinosaurus may have been as colorful and patterned as some of the snakes we see today.

Spinosaurus was closely related to *Baryonyx*, which we meet on page 88.

Spinosaurus fossils have been found in North Africa (in Egypt and Niger).

We are family

There was a great variety of size within dinosaur groups. *Spinosaurus* belonged to a group of dinosaurs called the spinosaurs. One of *Spinosaurus's* smallest relatives was a South American dinosaur called *Irritator*.

weird or what?

Irritator got its strange name after an irritating episode when its fossilized remains were altered by its finder in an attempt to make it more valuable.

Fossil remains of *Irritator* have been found in Brazil.

Yes, but it existed a lot earlier than *T. rex.*

A bright bulb?

Troodon is believed to have been the most intelligent of the dinosaurs, given the size of its brain in relation to its body.

Night hunter?

Scientists believe *Troodon* had good vision. It may even have had vertical pupils (just like a cat's) that would have helped it to hunt at night.

Model of male *Troodon*

Become an expert

on dinosaur eggs and nests, pages 22–23

Troodon's long slender limbs would have made it extremely agile.

A large sickle-shaped claw on *Troodon's* second toe was used to tear and slash.

Female *Troodon*

What might *Troodon* have hunted?

Let's look at a tooth

Troodon means "wounding tooth." The small teeth were serrated and hooked backward to help the *Troodon* grasp hold of prey.

Troodon tooth

A *Troodon* had about 120 teeth in its mouth. A human child has 20.

Troodon was probably feathered.

Grab and go

Troodon had three-fingered hands tipped with sharp claws that would have been ideal for grabbing and then holding onto its prey.

My nest!

There is evidence that *Troodon* lived in large colonies, caring for their young. Suspected *Troodon* nests found in Montana were 6 ft (2 m) wide and contained up to 24 eggs.

Probably baby dinosaurs, small mammals, snakes, lizards, and birds.

Meet the raptors

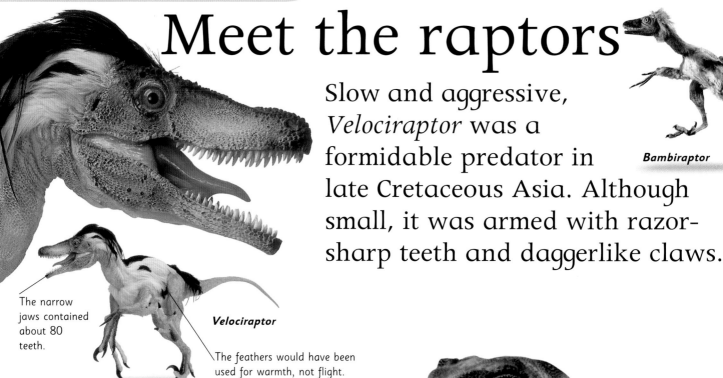

Slow and aggressive, *Velociraptor* was a formidable predator in late Cretaceous Asia. Although small, it was armed with razor-sharp teeth and daggerlike claws.

Bambiraptor

The narrow jaws contained about 80 teeth.

Velociraptor

The feathers would have been used for warmth, not flight.

A feathered dinosaur?

Some dinosaur fossils have been found with traces of a featherlike covering, and it's thought that *Velociraptor* may have had feathers, though no *Velociraptor* fossil has been found with them.

The killer claw

Deinonychus had a vicious killer claw on each of its hind legs. It held this off the ground but could slash it at victims.

Deinonychus

Experts believe that *Deinonychus* was one of the more intelligent dinosaurs.

Scientists now suspect *Deinoychus* was feathered, but the theory is so new that most models are naked.

Deinonychus foot fossil

What does the name *Velociraptor* mean?

Deinonychus

This skeleton has been mounted to show *Deinonychus* leaping toward a victim, claws ready.

Jump and grab

Velociraptor and its relations, such as the larger *Deinonychus*, probably hunted in packs and jumped onto the back of their prey, all four limbs extended.

Deinonychus means "terrible claw."

weird or what?
Velociraptor and *Deinonychus* belong to a group called the dromaeosaurids. Scientists believe these killing machines were related to the birds alive today.

Deinonychus had a lightweight body and long hind legs.

85

"Speedy thief." Scientists believe it may have reached 40 mph (65 km/h).

A pot-bellied dinosaur!

Is this the most bizarre of all the dinosaurs? *Therizinosaurus* certainly had the longest known arms, tipped with fingers that had claws up to 2 ft (60 cm) long.

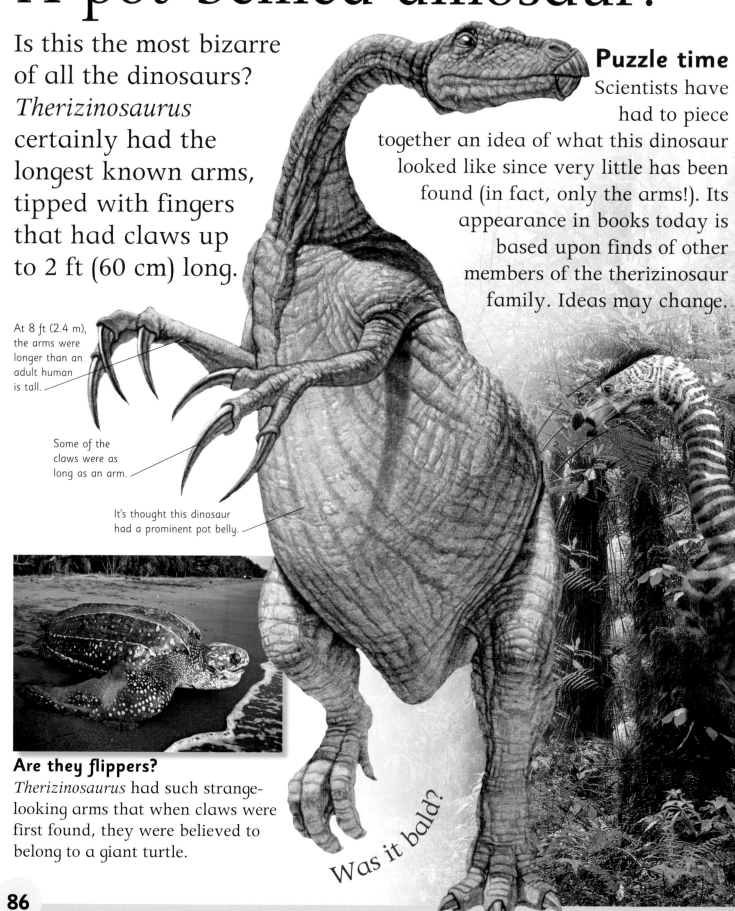

At 8 ft (2.4 m), the arms were longer than an adult human is tall.

Some of the claws were as long as an arm.

It's thought this dinosaur had a prominent pot belly.

Puzzle time
Scientists have had to piece together an idea of what this dinosaur looked like since very little has been found (in fact, only the arms!). Its appearance in books today is based upon finds of other members of the therizinosaur family. Ideas may change.

Are they flippers?
Therizinosaurus had such strange-looking arms that when claws were first found, they were believed to belong to a giant turtle.

Was it bald?

Do you think *Therizinosaurus* was a meat-eater or a plant-eater?

A strange cousin

Another odd-looking dinosaur from the same family as *Therizinosaurus* was *Beipiaosaurus*. Evidence shows that its arms and legs were covered with downy feathers.

Therizinosaurus may have had fine feathers, or it may have been bald. We don't know for certain.

It looks threatening, but its claws were blunt and it had a toothless beak. It ate plants.

Fish to eat

Ninety million years ago, a dinosaur stands watching, silently, by a large lake. Suddenly, claws flash in the sunlight, and a fish the length of your leg, a *Lepidotes*, is caught. Meet the fishing dinosaur, *Baryonyx*!

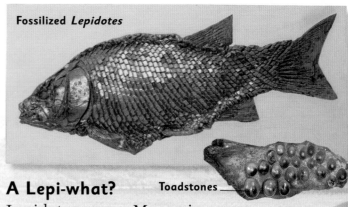

Fossilized *Lepidotes*

Toadstones

A Lepi-what?
Lepidotes was a Mesozoic fish that was found in lakes and shallow seas. Lepidotes teeth are a common fossil find in Southern England, where they are known as toadstones.

Did it really eat fish?
Baryonyx's crocodilelike jaws were perfect for grabbing fish, but we also know it ate fish because fossilized fish scales and bones were found with this dinosaur's fossil.

Baryonyx

How did toadstones get their name?

Look at that claw!

Baryonyx's name means "heavy claw." It was given this name because of its huge thumb claws. The long, curved claws were ideal for stabbing and snatching fish from the water.

Baryonyx's claw measures 12 in (30 cm) along the outside edge.

I found it first

The first fossilized claw of *Baryonyx* was found in England in the early 1980s by an amateur fossil collector named William Walker.

The jaw contains 96 pointed teeth.

Hidden secrets

After the claw was found, about 60 percent of the dinosaur was gradually uncovered in surrounding rocks, including this near perfect skull.

Fossilized *Baryonyx* skull

Hundreds of years ago people thought they came from the heads of living toads!

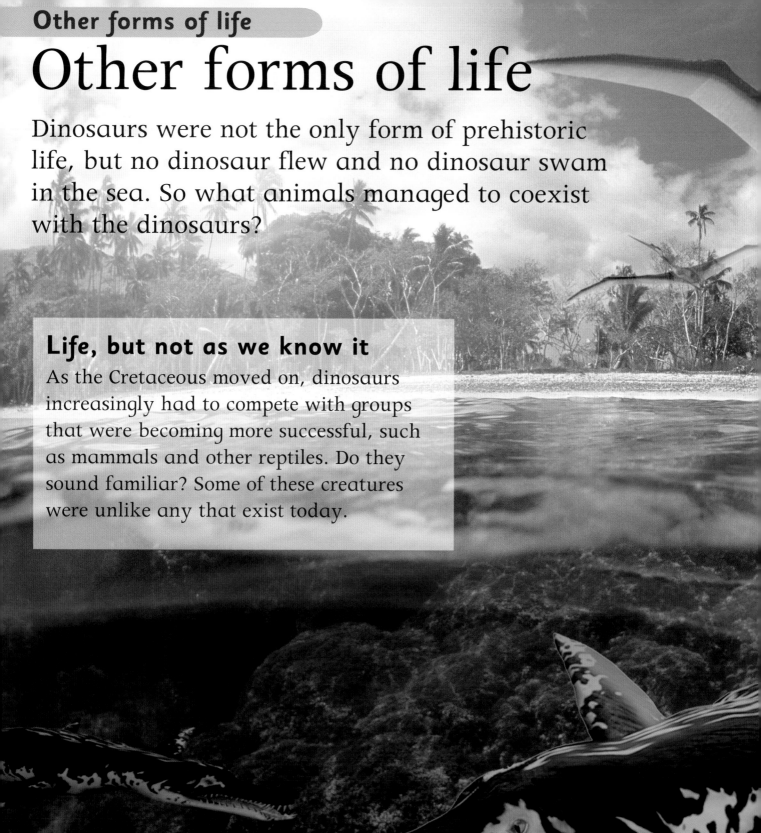

Other forms of life

Dinosaurs were not the only form of prehistoric life, but no dinosaur flew and no dinosaur swam in the sea. So what animals managed to coexist with the dinosaurs?

Life, but not as we know it

As the Cretaceous moved on, dinosaurs increasingly had to compete with groups that were becoming more successful, such as mammals and other reptiles. Do they sound familiar? Some of these creatures were unlike any that exist today.

Would dinosaurs have eaten pterosaurs?

Curiosity quiz
Look through the Other forms of life pages to identify each of the picture clues below.

Pterosaur

Plesiosaur

Become an expert

on pterosaurs, pages **94–95**

on plesiosaurs, pages **92–93**

Yes, if they managed to catch them!

Monsters of the deep

There may have been no marine dinosaurs, but a frightening variety of toothed giant reptiles ruled the seas while the dinosaurs ruled the land.

Ichthyosaurus

Elasmosaurus

Elasmosaurus was air-breathing, just like whales today.

Ichthyosaurs had huge eyes.

Its neck was as long as its body and tail

Swim away...

An *Ichthyosaurus* moves swiftly to keep from being eaten. The swimming ichthyosaurs, including *Ichthyosaurus* itself, were perfectly suited for chasing fast-moving prey, such as squid, but were vulnerable to attack from larger marine reptiles.

... from danger!

Watch out! A *Liopleurodon* is attacking the ichthyosaurs from below. Perhaps the largest sea-based predator of all time, *Liopleurodon* was a short-necked plesiosaur.

92

What did *Liopleurodon* eat?

What's that?

Elasmosaurus was also a plesiosaur, but it was long-necked. Its four paddle-shaped limbs propelled it easily through the water. It grew up to 46 ft (14 m) in length.

I recognize that!

Many Mesozoic occupants of the Earth's seas would be familiar to us.

 Jellyfish have been around for about 400 million years.

 Corals are fragile animals, but they have managed to survive since the dinosaurs.

 The **great white shark**'s ancestors date back to the Cretaceous period.

 Squid were on the menu for ichthyosaurs, shown by fossil evidence.

Snails are also present in fossil form, showing they too are great survivors.

Liopleurodon may have reached 80 ft (25 m).

Liopleurodon

weird or what?

Some people think the "monster" in Loch Ness, a Scottish Lake, is a pleisaur trapped there when the sea receded millions of years ago!

The daggerlike teeth were twice as long as those of *T. rex*.

Anything it could catch, including pterosaurs that flew too close to the water's surface.

Monsters of the air

No dinosaur flew, but they had relatives that did: the pterosaurs, or flying reptiles. Some were tiny, but others had the wingspan of a small airplane.

Who came first?

Early pterosaurs had long tails and narrow wings. They were fairly small—*Dimorphodon* and *Rhamphorhynchus* were about 3 ft (1 m) in length.

The tail was used to control the direction of flight.

Rhamphorhynchus

Dimorphodon

Dimorphodon had a large, puffinlike head, with a toothed beak.

What did they eat?

Lots of pterosaur fossils have been found in coastal areas, suggesting they swooped low over the sea, picking off fish. They probably also caught insects.

94

Were pterosaurs a type of bird?

Pterodactylus

Look at mine!
Many Cretaceous pterosaurs had crests. They may have been used to attract mates.

Tropeognathus had a large crest at the end of its upper jaw.

Anhanguera had a crest on its upper and lower jaw.

Pteranodon had a long, backward-pointing crest.

Dsungaripterus had two crests on the top of its head.

Did they have fur?
Some pterosaurs may have had fur, like modern-day bats. They also had large eyes, giving them excellent vision.

Tropeognathus

It's the size of a plane!
A male *Tropeognathus* may have had a 20 ft (6 m) wingspan, though it weighed less than a seven-year-old child.

The wings were made of skin that grew between an extra long fourth finger bone and the leg.

Who was the biggest?
By the Cretaceous period, pterosaurs had got bigger. Possibly the largest flying reptile of all was found in Texas in the 1930s. *Quetzalcoatlus* had a wingspan of 40–46 ft (12–14 m).

Quetzalcoatlus

95

No. Pterosaurs were winged reptiles and were not related to birds.

Were there mammals?

Mammals began to appear in the late Cretaceous period, but they were small and were dominated by the success of the dinosaurs. Ultimately, they were to become incredibly successful, but it took millions of years.

Are they really that small?

Primitive mammals began to appear in the late Triassic, some 220 million years ago, and they were tiny. Just look at the mammal timeline shown below with its comparison to the size of an adult human's hand! These mammals were probably nocturnal, hiding in leaf litter and hunting for insects and maybe even dinosaur eggs.

Size guide	220 mya	208 mya	150 mya	83.5 to 71 mya	70 mya
	Eozostrodon	Sinoconodon	Docodon	Zalambdalestes	Alphadon
	Triassic: 248 to 206 million years ago		Jurassic: 206 to 144 million years ago	Cretaceous: 144 to 65 million years ago	
	MESOZOIC ERA 248 to 65 million years ago (mya)				

Early mammals probably raided dinosaur eggs if they had the chance.

Why would early mammals have been nocturnal?

When did mammals get big?

The first large predatory mammals, the creodonts, didn't emerge until Paleocene times, the period of time after the extinction of the dinosaurs.

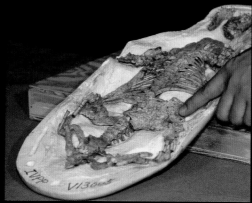

Did mammals eat dinosaurs?

Paleontologists recently found a fossilized *Repenomamus*, a badger-sized beast. That's enormous for a Mesozoic mammal! It even had the remains of baby dinosaurs in its gut.

That looks like...

Another early mammal was the platypuslike *Steropodon*. Like the platypus today, these mammals probably laid eggs.

Early mammals walked on all fours, had long tails, and long bodies and snouts.

Docodon

weird or what?

Dinosaurs were amazingly successful: they ruled Earth for 180 million years. Humans emerged some 200,000 years ago. That's a tiny amount of geological time.

This would have allowed them to avoid being eaten by reptiles and dinosaurs.

Size matters

The creatures that lived during the Mesozoic Era varied dramatically in size—some were tiny, but others grew to enormous proportions.

That's not so big...
Ichthyosaurs varied in size. Some were as small as your arm, while many were the size of a dolphin.

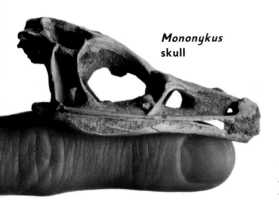

Mononykus skull

Is that its skull?
Some dinosaurs were really small. This little dinosaur's skull is shown life-size.

... but that's a giant!
However, in Triassic times, ichthyosaurs reached massive proportions.

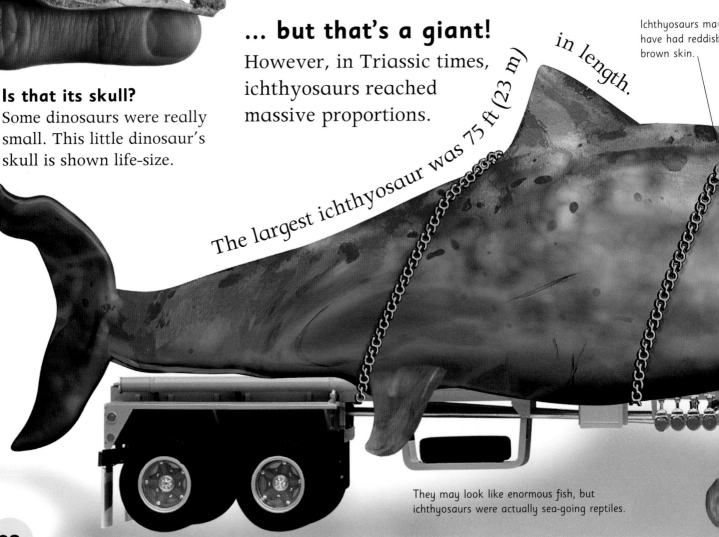

The largest ichthyosaur was 75 ft (23 m) in length.

Ichthyosaurs may have had reddish brown skin.

They may look like enormous fish, but ichthyosaurs were actually sea-going reptiles.

Was the largest ichthyosaur longer than a blue whale?

Archelon fossil

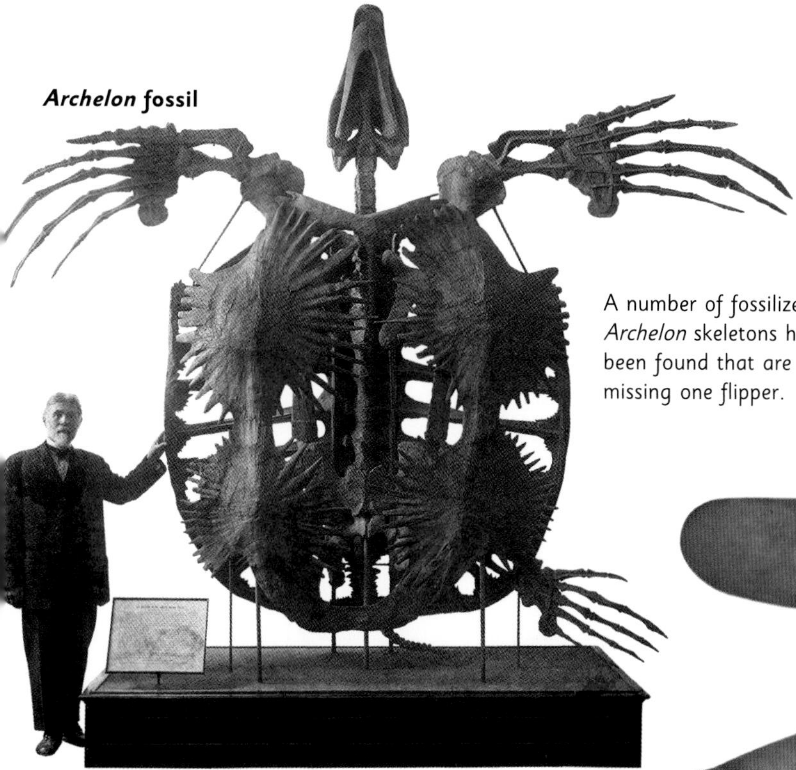

A number of fossilized *Archelon* skeletons have been found that are missing one flipper.

That's not a turtle!

Archelon was a turtle, but it was three times the size of the largest turtle today. Fully grown adults had 13 ft- (4 m-) long shells.

It's a tiny opossum

Alphadon was one of the first marsupials; these animals carry their young in pouches. Kangaroos are also marsupials. But *Alphadon* was tiny.

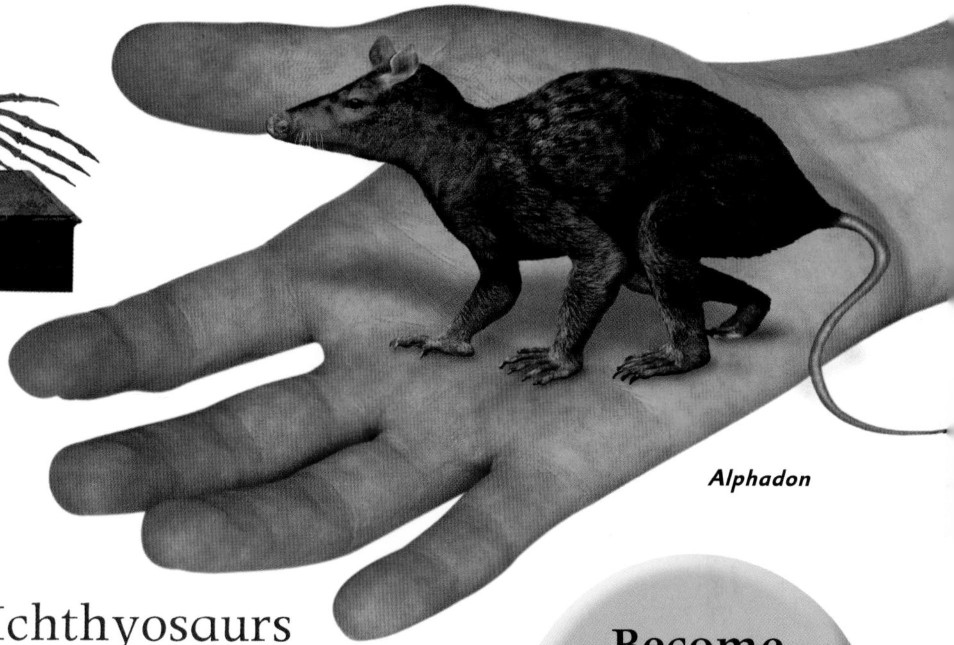

Alphadon

It lived 210 million years ago.

Ichthyosaurs are one of the best-known of all Mesozoic creatures.

Become an expert

on ichthyosaurs, page 92

Ichthyosaur

No. They were big, but blue whales reach 100 ft (30 m) in length.

Fossils

Fossils have been found all over the world, but they are not easy to recognize and are often discovered by accident, perhaps following construction work.

The right conditions?

Lots of fossils have been found, but for every fossilized dinosaur, hundreds and thousands died, decayed, and left no trace. Fossilization requires certain conditions.

"Fossil" comes from the Latin word *fossilis*. It means "dug up."

Fossils are encased in rock that has to be carefully removed.

Name one difference between fossilization and mummification.

What kind of fossil is that?

There are different types of fossils. Classification depends on how they were created.

Total preservation:
This is when the whole animal is preserved, such as an insect in amber.

Semipreservation:
This results when just the hard parts of an object are preserved unaltered.

Petrified:
Wood is sometimes petrified. It means the hard parts are preserved, but are chemically altered.

Natural mold:
This occurs when the animal or plant decays away leaving a hole in the rock. The paleontologist fills this with latex rubber.

Natural cast:
Forms as a mold, but the hole is filled by natural substances. For example, a fossil may be cast in a stone called flint.

Trace fossils:
These are fossils that show where an animal has been, such as footprints, nests, or coprolites (animal dung).

Curiosity quiz

Look through the Fossils pages to identify each of the picture clues below.

Become an expert
on how a dinosaur may turn into a fossil, pages 102–103

Fossils are preserved in Earth's rocks. Mummification is usually done by people.

How was it made?

Fossils may form when animal or plant matter is buried soon after death under mud or sand. However, that's just the beginning of a process that takes millions of years.

70 million years ago
A *T. rex* has died and is washed downstream. It rests on layers of soft mud and is rapidly buried.

Five years later
The creature's soft flesh has slowly rotted away, leaving the bones. Over time these begin to move apart.

50 million years ago
A sea has now spread over the area once occupied by the river. Heavy pressure is slowly turning the sand to sandstone.

Can you name some of the things that fossilize?

Two million years ago

The passing of millions of years has seen mountain ranges rising above the fossilized *T. rex*, but gradually they are being worn down by extreme weather.

Last year

The area around the fossil is now a desert. Two walkers investigate further when they see the exposed tip of a fossilized bone.

Today

Paleontologists are now hard at work, uncovering the rest of the *T. rex*. The bones will be removed one by one. The skeleton may end up in a museum.

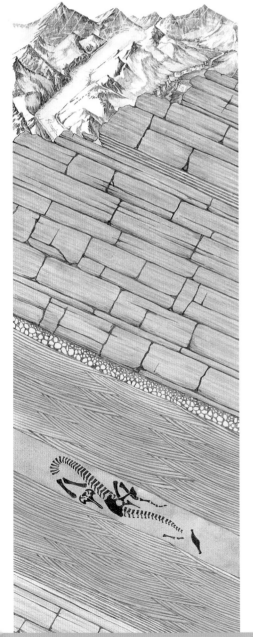

Fossils include bones, teeth, footprints, and skin impressions. Plants also fossilize.

Masses of bones

Certain places are rich in dinosaur fossils. In some areas, dinosaurs may have been drowned in floods; in others they look like they were caught in traps where many dinosaurs died at about the same time. We can learn a lot from these "dinosaur traps".

What's been found?

Paleontologists studied one dinosaur trap in Utah and discovered more than 10,000 bones. They believe the plant-eaters stopped to drink at a lake and were trapped in deep mud. Predators were trapped when they approached in the hope of an easy meal.

A paleontologist investigates one fossil in a wall of fossils formed when lots of dinosaurs drowned in the same place.

What we can learn

Fossils can tell us how large an animal was, what it ate, and even how it may have died.

An Allosaurus tries to attack a Stegosaurus.

What is a predator?

Ichthyosaur dropping, or coprolite.

Fish scales

What we can't learn
Although dinosaur skin impressions exist, we have no way of knowing what color dinosaurs really were.

Dinosaur skin impression

This one ate fish!
Fossilized droppings can tell us what an animal ate. Ichthyosaurs swam in oceans while dinosaurs ruled the land. This fossilized ichthyosaur dropping has clear fish scales.

Could *T. rex* have been this colorful?

A complete find?
When paleontologists discover a new dinosaur fossil site, they refer to the bones they find in one of four ways.

 Articulated skeleton. This is a skeleton that is still joined together as it was in life. In rare cases it is almost complete.

 Associated skeleton. This is where the bones have been broken apart and spread out, but are obviously from the same animal.

 Isolated bone. This is an individual bone that has been separated from the skeleton. It may be a skull or a femur.

Float is what paleontologists call the scraps of bone that are too small to be of use.

Both will be stuck in mud and die.

After 145 million years, the predator trap is discovered and the fossils exposed.

A predator is an animal that hunts and kills another animal.

Investigating a find

It takes an incredibly long time to excavate and examine a fossil find. Sometimes bones are in sand, but usually they have to be removed from rock, which is chipped away in small sections. It all has to go.

Easy does it!

If a skeleton is discovered, most of it may be covered with an immense amount of rock and dirt, which has to be cleared away. It's a skillful job, since no one wants to damage the fossil.

Paleontologists investigating the site of a new find.

Grid control

It is important that the location and position of the bones are recorded accurately. That's why you'll often see a string grid above a find, so a chart can be mapped.

Can you think how a large fossil might be moved once it has its plaster coating?

Don't break it!
At the site, large fossils will be wrapped in bandages and liquid plaster. This will set hard to protect the fossil before it can be moved to a museum, where it can be cleaned and examined.

The fossil is wrapped in plaster bandages.

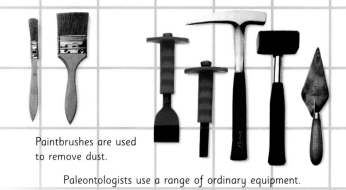

Paintbrushes are used to remove dust.

Paleontologists use a range of ordinary equipment.

Tools of the trade
You'd find that a paleontologist's toolbox is pretty ordinary, with hammers, trowels, and paintbrushes.

Paleontologists are dinosaur detectives.

The work doesn't stop
Back at the museum, the plaster cast is removed and the fossil examined. It requires patience. It took technicians more than 3,500 hours (about five months) to clean and repair this one *T. rex* skull. Then a cast was made for exhibition.

A large fossil might be lifted out by helicopter.

Is it real?

Fossil exhibits in museums are sometimes replicas, since these are lighter in weight and the original fossil can then remain in protective storage. So how is the replica made?

It all begins with the bones

First of all, a mold is made of the fossilized bone. It's done by painting liquid rubber onto the fossil's surface.

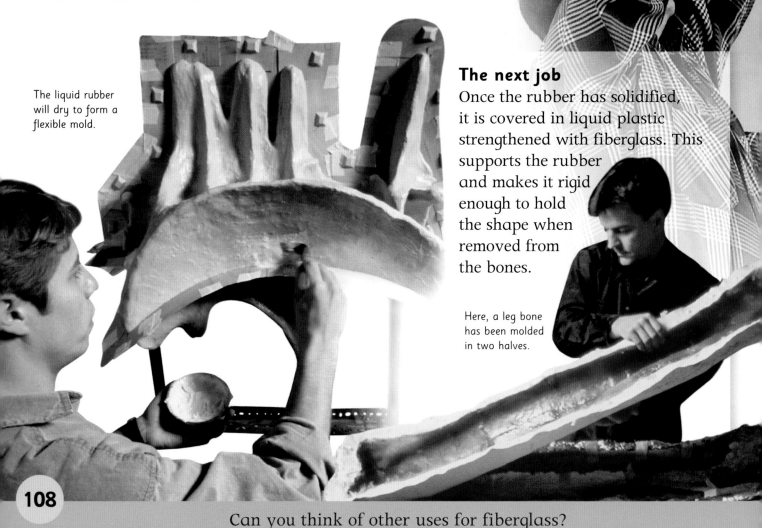

The liquid rubber will dry to form a flexible mold.

The next job

Once the rubber has solidified, it is covered in liquid plastic strengthened with fiberglass. This supports the rubber and makes it rigid enough to hold the shape when removed from the bones.

Here, a leg bone has been molded in two halves.

Can you think of other uses for fiberglass?

An *Allosaurus* gets its head in a museum exhibit.

Ready to show!

The finished bones are now ready to display. A complete skeleton will be assembled in sections before these sections are brought together. The whole operation takes careful planning.

Become an expert

on assembling the *Barosaurus* for display, pages 110–111

Filling up the molds

The shape is then filled with liquid plastic. This will set hard, forming a stiff but lightweight foam. The replica bones need to be light in weight.

Liquid plastic is poured into the mold.

Let's take a look!

Once the plastic has set, the outer molds are carefully removed. Any joins are filed to smooth them, and the foam plastic replica bone, or cast, will then be painted to match the original fossil.

The cast is easily removed from its mold.

Fiberglass is strong but also lightweight, which makes it perfect for boats and cars.

It's a jigsaw

After fossilized bones have been studied and replicas have been made, a museum may decide to mount a display for people to come and see. It can be a long process.

Stick to the plans

There are a lot of bones in a large dinosaur, and specialists have to be careful to get each bone in the right place.

Ready with the ribs

Sometimes parts of the skeleton's frame are assembled elsewhere and then transported to the museum.

Bring in the machines

Some museums are fortunate enough to have high ceilings, perfect for exhibiting a rearing sauropod, as here. This *Barosaurus* skeleton was so large, it needed the help of two cherry pickers to position the sections.

When finished, this replica will be more than 49 ft (15 m) high.

2352

How many bones were put together to make the *Barosaurus* skeleton?

Almost done

If a display is ambitious, as here, it may need support from metal rods, which have to be welded in position. After all, no one wants it to fall on a visitor's head!

A welder is protected from sparks by a flame-resistant helmet and gloves.

The finished display shows the mother *Barosaurus* rearing to protect her young from an approaching *Allosaurus*.

111

End of the dinosaurs

The last 10 million years of the Cretaceous period saw a huge variety of dinosaurs. They were flourishing. Yet the age of the dinosaurs was coming to an end.

What is the most commonly accepted theory for the end of the dinosaurs?

Why did they die?

Numerous theories have been put forward for why the dinosaurs died out. Some are possibilities, while others are kind of silly.

 Plague wiped out millions of people in 1300s' Europe. Did dinosaurs get sick?

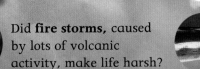 Did **fire storms,** caused by lots of volcanic activity, make life harsh?

Meteorites from space may have brought widespread devastation.

 Egg predators increased. Did fewer and fewer dinosaur babies survive?

 Tsunami created by earthquakes and meteorites destroyed habitats.

 Ice ages have resulted in huge changes—but there was no ice age at that time.

Lack of sleep is one of the sillier theories put forward for the end of the dinosaurs.

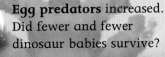

Curiosity quiz

Look through the End of the dinosaurs pages to identify each of the picture clues below.

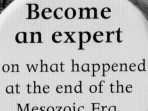

Become an expert

on what happened at the end of the Mesozoic Era, pages 114–115

The most likely theory is that it was the result of an immense meteorite hitting Earth.

What happened?

Sixty-five million years ago the dinosaurs died out, along with the pterosaurs and the plesiosaurs. It was a mass extinction, but what was the cause? Many believe it was the result of a meteorite.

What changed?

Scientists now believe a massive meteorite hit Earth, creating a dust cloud of noxious fumes that screened out the Sun and changed the climate.

Who died?

The extinction saw the loss of huge numbers of animals, including:

Pterosaurs, which had once filled the skies with their airborne acrobatics.

Dinosaurs, which had evolved into a huge variety of types.

Huge reptiles, which disappeared from the oceans.

The rock would have hit Earth's crust with terrific force, sending shockwaves around the world.

It was a big one!
In the early1990s, geologists found the remains of a massive crater in Mexico. It was 112 miles (180 km) wide. They believe it was caused by a meteorite smashing into Earth 65 million years ago.

How big were the animals that survived the extinction?

Was that all?

The meteorite hit at a time of immense volcanic activity in what is now western India. This activity would have sent up clouds of ash and dust that would have blocked the Sun's light—just like the effect of the meteorite. That's two major events around the same time.

The rock that created the Mexican crater was 6 miles (10 km) in diameter.

From meteorite to volcano, the extinction may have been a combination of conditions.

An exploding volcano sends up clouds of lethal dust.

No land animal heavier than a large dog survived.

End of the dinosaurs
Who survived?

It may have been a catastrophic event for the dinosaurs, but incredibly, some creatures did survive the dinosaur extinction.

They made it!

Among the animals that survived were sharks, jellyfish, fish, scorpions, birds, and insects.

Tiny mammals survived the event that killed the dinosaurs.

Shark

Jellyfish

I was there at the end
Fossil records show us that *Triceratops* was one of the last of the dinosaurs, along with *T. rex*.

An ancient history
Tuataras, curiously spiny reptiles that live on islands off New Zealand, are related to reptiles that were around at the time of the dinosaurs.

The tuatara did too!

Tuatara

Which era came after the Mesozoic Era?

Scaly survivors

Although no large land animals made it, a number of smaller reptiles did outlive the dinosaurs.

Egyptian vulture

Snakes There are now some 2,900 different types of snake.

Turtles first appeared about 200 million years ago, before the dinosaurs!

Lizards There are about 4,500 different lizards. They enjoy huge success.

Crocodiles largely inhabit freshwater rivers and lakes.

Birds of prey are the most successful predators of all birds.

Birds did!

Become an expert

on the link between birds and dinosaurs,
pages 118–119

The Cenozoic Era, which saw the rise of the mammals.

Living dinosaurs

You may think that reptiles have more in common with dinosaurs, but dinosaurs may be more closely related to birds!

A hidden link?

The link between dinosaurs and birds is a puzzle. *Caudipteryx* appears to have been a combination of bird and dinosaur.

Caudipteryx

Caudipteryx would not have been able to fly since its wings were too small.

Fossilized *Archaeopteryx*

The first bird?

The earliest-known bird is *Archaeopteryx*, which first appeared in the Jurassic. It had the toothed head, clawed fingers, and long bony tail of a dinosaur, but it also had feathers.

Archaeopteryx means "ancient wing."

What size do you think *Archaeopteryx* reached?

Why feathers?

Feathers protect birds from water and from temperature changes, and they may have evolved on some dinosaurs for the same purpose.

Caudipteryx was a Cretaceous creature.

Feathers provide good insulation from cold.

Caudipteryx had clawed hands. It also had teeth.

Hoatzin are found in parts of South America.

We have claws

Some modern birds have clawed wings. Hoatzin chicks have two tiny claws at the end of each wing. These are not used in the adult, but the chicks use them to clamber through trees.

weird or what? There were undoubtedly feathered dinosaurs, but paleontologists continue to debate the possible link between dinosaurs and birds. It does seem unlikely, though, that any dinosaur flew.

Caudipteryx was about the size of a turkey.

Sinosauropteryx

Pieces of a puzzle

More and more "dino-birds" are being discovered, and each discovery helps our understanding. This model is based on feathered fossils found in China.

It was small—about the size of a pigeon.

Dinosaur records

The biggest... the smallest... the longest... the tallest... Here are the dinosaur record breakers!

Mussaurus

As long as a pencil, this young *Mussaurus* lived in the desert lands of Triassic South America. Its name means "mouse lizard".

Smallest dinosaur found: A skeleton of a *Mussaurus* was 8 in (20 cm) long—though it was only a baby.

Longest neck: *Mamenchisaurus's* neck was 46–49 ft (14–15 m) long—about the same as three elephants in a row.

Tallest dinosaur: *Sauroposeidon* stood at a height of 60 ft (18 m)—about as tall as three giraffes standing on top of each other.

Longest tail: *Diplodocus's* tail was just a little shorter—around 43–46 ft (13–14 m) long.

Longest dinosaur: the nose of a *Seismosaurus* was 130–165 ft (40–50 m) from the end of its tail.

Largest claw: The claws of a *Therizinosaurus* grew to 36 in (91 cm) long—about as long as a man's arm.

Biggest meat-eating dinosaur: The 50 ft- (15 m-) long *Giganotosaurus* must have been a terrifying predator!

Largest egg: *Macroelongatoolithus xixiaensis* eggs found in China were 18 in (46 cm) long.

Most teeth: Hadrosaurs, such as *Lambeosaurus,* had more than 1,000 teeth—all for chewing plants!

Largest head: Both *Pentaceratops* and *Torosaurus* had heads more than 10 ft (3 m) long.

Smallest adult dinosaur: A fully grown adult *Microraptor* was around 16 in (40 cm) long.

Pentaceratops

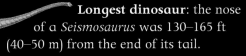

Is this the only creature that has sat on its eggs for 80 million years?

One *Oviraptor* died on its nest.

Will these dinosaur records ever change?

T. rex was among the biggest meat-eaters ever—but it was still smaller than Giganotosaurus.

Life-size model of *T. rex*

The first *Iguanodon* skeletons were found in Belgium, by coal miners.

Smallest brain: *Stegosaurus* had a brain the size of three table-tennis balls.

Fastest dinosaur: It is thought that *Dromiceiomimus* reached speeds of 45 mph (70 kph).

Earliest dinosaur: *Eoraptor* lived about 228 million years ago, in the Triassic period.

First herd found: the first big collection of dinosaur skeletons was found in 1878. There were 32 skeletons, all of *Iguanodon*.

They might! New dinosaur fossils are being discovered all the time.

Glossary

Articulated Things that are joined together, such as the bones of a skeleton.

Cold-blooded An animal that cannot maintain its body temperature and has to rely on the Sun's heat to warm up, or find shade in which to cool down. Reptiles are cold-blooded.

Geologist A person who studies the Earth and its rocks.

Habitat The place in which a group of animals and plants live. It could be a desert or a city park.

Herbivore An animal that eats plants.

Apatosaurus

Apatosaurus was a sauropod. It thrived 150 million years ago in the Jurassic period.

Continent One of Earth's huge land masses, like Asia. There are seven continents.

Coprolite Fossilized dinosaur droppings.

Cretaceous The geological name given to the period between 144 and 65 million years ago.

Extinction The dying out of an animal or plant species.

Fossil The remains of animal or plant matter that has been preserved in Earth's crust.

Jurassic The geological name given to the period between 206 and 144 million years ago.

Mammal A warm-blooded animal that has a backbone and also drinks milk from its mother.

Mesozoic Era The major division of geological time (called an era) when the dinosaurs lived. It contains the Triassic, Jurassic, and Cretaceous periods.

Meteorite A lump of rock that falls to Earth from space.

122

Nocturnal An animal that is active at night and sleeps during the day.

Palaeontologist Someone who removes animal and plant fossils from the ground and studies them.

Trace fossil A fossil that indicates where an animal has been, but is not part of the animal's remains. Fossilized footprints are trace fossils.

Warm-blooded An animal that can maintain its body temperature by using food as fuel to generate heat. Humans are warm-blooded.

Triassic The geological name given to the period between 248 and 206 million years ago.

Vertebra One of the bones that link together to form an animal's backbone, or spine.

Predator An animal that hunts and kills other animals for food.

Tsunami A huge wave caused by movements in the Earth's crust. The cause, for example, may be a deep-sea earthquake.

Sauropod The name for a group of large, plant-eating dinosaurs. Sauropods had long necks and tails and bulky bodies.

Scavenger An animal that feeds on the dead bodies of other animals.

Species A group of animals or plants that share the same characteristics.

Theropod The group name for meat-eating dinosaurs.

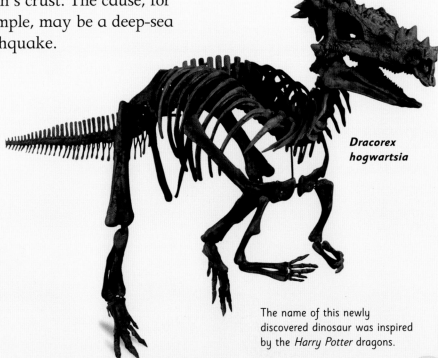

Dracorex hogwartsia

The name of this newly discovered dinosaur was inspired by the *Harry Potter* dragons.

Index

Can you recognize and name any of the dinosaur silhouettes? Turn to the next page to check your answers...

Reference section

How many
dinosaurs on the
previous page did
you manage
to name?

Plateosaurus

Thecodontosaurus

Herrerasaurus

Compsognathus

Brachiosaurus

Stegosaurus

Spinosaurus

Velociraptor

Iguanodon

Lesothosaurus

Triceratops

Protoceratops

Euoplocephalus

T. rex

Picture credits

The publisher would like to thank the following for their kind permission to reproduce their photographs:

(Key: a-above; b-below/bottom; c-centre; l-left; r-right; t-top)

Alamy Images: Jeff Morgan 72b; Werner Otto 126b, 127b; **American Museum Of Natural History:** 47c, 87tl; **Ardea:** Francois Gohier 22br, 58cr, 59cr; **Karen Carr:** 35br; **The Children's Museum of Indianapolis:** 123br; CM Studio: 1r, 34cl, 36tl, 42-43c, 55c, 57cra, 59tr, 81tr, 126bl, 128; **Corbis:** Gary Bell 90-91c; Bettmann 46tl; Jonathan Blair 33tr, 36-37bc; Gary Braasch 80-81cb; James D'Addio / Beateworks 10tr; Terry W. Eggers 37crb; Sandy Felsenthal 1bl; Darrell Gulin 14tc; Wolfgang Kaehler 80cl; Layne Kennedy 107clb; Macduff Everton 47tl; Charles Mauzy 46ca; Buddy Mays 69cra; Richard T. Nowitz 4-5c, 106cb; Greg Probst 66-67bc; Louie Psihoyos 15crb, 22cl, 22cr, 26tr, 39br, 41tl, 67cra, 68tr, 77tr; Reuters 77br; Reuters / Peter Morgan 54cr; ML Sinibaldi 62-63c (background); Jon Sparks 38tr; Jim Zuckerman 51tr; **Tom Dempsey / www.photoseek.com:** 48-49c; **Frank DeNota:** 67crb, 83c; **DK Images:** American Museum of Natural History 20fcra, 21ca; Angus Beare 113cl; Simone Boni/L.R. Galante 70fcl; Centaur Studios 7fbr, 12fcla, 20tc; Centaur Studios/Andy Crawford 126fbr; Peter Chadwick 35fbr, 84fbl, 85br; Jim Channell 120ftr; Brian Cosgrove 37tc; Bedrock Studios 4bl, 5bl, 19fcr, 39fcl, 57tc, 57bl, 78fbl, 120fcrb, 126fbl; Courtesy of Dinosaur State Park, Connecticut 101fbl; Courtesy of the |Natural History Museum, London 6868fcl; Courtesy of the American Museum of Natural HIstory 68fcl, 73fcrb, 108ftr, 108fbl, 108fbr, 109fbl, 109fbr, 110ftr, 110fclb, 111fcra, 111fcl; Courtesy of the Carnegie Museum of Natural History, Pittsburgh 123fcl; Courtesy of the Field Museum, Chicago 65bc; Courtesy of the Institute of Geology and Palaeontology, Tubingen, Germany 39fcr; Courtesy of the Museo Arentino De Cirendas Naterales, Buenos Aires 75ca; Courtesy of The National Birds of Prey Centre, Gloucestershire 113fcrb, 117fcr; Courtesy of the National Museum of Natural History, Smithsonian Institution 57ftl; Courtesy of the Natural History Museum, London 11bl, 13fcrb, 15fcr, 113cla, 119cla, 120fcr; Courtesy of the Natural History Museum,

London / Colin Keates 15c, 18fcl, 21cla; Courtesy of the Royal Tyrell Museum 13fbr; Courtesy of the Royal Tyrrell Museum of Palaeontology, Alberta 65fcr; Courtesy of the Royal Tyrrell Museum of Palaeontology, Alberta, Canada 75fcr, 120fclb; Courtesy of The Sedgewick Museum of Geology, Cambridge 101fcl; Courtesy of the Senckenberg Nature Museum, Frankfurt 65br, 118bl; Courtesy of the State Museum of Nature, Stuttgart 33fcrb, 65fcrb, 105fcra; James Stevenson 19br; Roby Braun 4fbr, 12cb, 17fcr, 17ftr, 73cl, 121cr, 126bc, 126br, 127fbl; Courtsey of Royal Tyrell Museum 69fclb; Andy Crawford 16, 39cla; Andy Crawford/Royal Tyrell Museum 28fcl; Dave King 20tl, 120fcra; David Donkin 9bl, 9br; Donks Models 11ftr; Christine M. Douglas 45ftr, 57fbr; Philip Dowell 10fbl, 10bl, 22bl; Mike Dunning 11fcbr; Neil Fletcher / Matthew Ward 57fcra; Giuliano Fornari 114cra, 114crb; Christopher & Sally Gable 25bc; Steve Gorton 57fcrb; Steve Gorton / John Holmes 74cb, 75clb; Jonathan Hateley 27fcl, 113fcra, 118cr, 119clb; Nigel Hicks 11fbr; Graham High, Centaur Studios 4br, 5fbl, 12c, 29bc, 68bc, 69bc, 114cr, 126crb, 127bl, 127br; John Holmes 25ftl, 29fcr, 127bc; Jon Hughes 34-35b, 35tl, 43tr, 44-45c, 53cr, 56c, 57b, 60c, 61r, 63c, 79cr, 88-89c; Jeremy Hunt 95fcr; Colin Keates 101cla, 101cb; Colin Keates / Courtesy of The Natural History Museum, London 31fcr, 31fcrb, 54cra, 56ftr; Colin Keates / Natural History Museum, London 17fcrb; Gary Kevin 24fcrb, 25fcrb; Gunter Marx 113clb; Ray Moller 10fcl; Frank Greenaway 11br, 14, 95ftr, 95fcrb, 116ca, 116c, 116cb; Natural History Museum, London 24fbl, 29fbr, 31fcra; Stepehen Oliver 99br; Gary Ombler 4bc, 20tr, 27fbl, 63cra, 71crb, 79fcl, 99fcra, 119cb, 127fbr; Gary Ombler, Graham High 127cb; Lloyd Park 59tc, 117fbl; Peabody Museum of Natural History, Yale University 84fclb, 85tc; Peabody Museum of Natural History, Yale University / Lynton Gardiner 84bl; David Peart 116fcl; Miguel Periera 45bc; Roger Phillips 38fbl, 43fcra; Luis Rey 84tl, 84ftl; Rough guides 15ftr, 127c; Karl Shone 113fcr, 116fbl; Steve Shott 95fcra; Staab Studios 120fbr; John Temperton 55fcra, 56fcra, 121crb; Cecile Treal & Jean-Michel Ruiz 11fcr; Matthew Ward 32fcla, 41ftr, 53fcrb; Laura Wickenden 117ftl; James Young 71ftr; Jerry Young 11cr (Scrubland), 14cl, 20cra, 113fbr, 117fclb; **FLPA:** Flip de Nooyer / Foto Natura 119tr, 119tc; **Getty Images:** 77c; AFP / William West 61tl; Theo Allofs 60-61cb (background); Jack Dvkinga

34bc; Rich Frishman 107br; David Hiser 64bl; Brian Kenney 21clb; Raimund Koch 38tl (Background); Timothy Laman / National Geographic 27ca; Klaus Nigge 78-79c (background); Panoramic Images 42l, 43cr, 55c, 68-69bc; Louie Psihoyos 105tl, 105crb, 106cra, 107tl, 120cr, 121c; James Randklev 40-41tc; Scott Sady 28-29tc; Miguel Salmeron 26-27bc; Science Faction / Louie Psihoyos 64, 100b, 103t; Pankai & Insy Shah 26-27 (wadi); Andreas Stirnberg 48-49c; Hans Strand 82l, 83br; Steffen Thalemann 44-45b; **Kokoro Dinosaurs:** 2-3, 119br, 120bc; **The Natural History Museum, London,** 5br, 6tl, 6cl, 6-7bc, 13crb, 18br, 19cb, 20cr, 21cl, 23bc, 24cl, 25cra, 27tl, 32bl, 67br, 83tl, 88tr, 89c, 120clb, 120cl, 120cla, 120fbl; Anness Publishing 120fcla, 120fcl; De Agostini 54tr; **NHPA / Photoshot:** Andrea & Antonella Ferrari 70-71cb; Jonathan & Angela Scott 34clb; **OSF / photolibrary:** 88cl; Highlights for Children 40bl, 45tc, 45tr; **Reuters:** Peter Morgan 97tc; Ho New 97cra; **Science Faction Images:** Louie Psihoyos 13cra, 18bl, 22cl (background), 23cr, 23tl, 24cra, 31tl, 42clb, 50-51bc, 53tl, 67cr, 79bl, 84-85c, 98cl; **Science Photo Library:** Hervé Conge, ISM 69tl; Christian Darkin 8c, 13cla, 30tr, 30-31c, 73t, 97cla; Bernhard Edmaier 115cr; Carlos Goldin 78tr; Gary Hincks 36-37crb; NASA 114bc; Laurie O'Keefe 50clb; David Parker 76-77c; D. Van Ravensswaay 114clb; Joe Tucciarone 86cr; **Mineo Shiraishi:** 53c, 81b; **Still Pictures:** Kelvin Aitken 86l; John Cancalosi / Peter Arnold. Inc. 1cl, 23tc; **SuperStock:** J. Silver 21br; **US Geological Survey Western Region:** 11cl; **Special Collections Department, J. Willard Marriott Library, University of Utah:** 65tl; **Warren Photographic:** 32-33, 72t, 112-113c, 116tr; Jane Burton 94bc; **Kevin Wasden (kevinwasden.com):** 53cb; **Yale University Peabody Museum Of Natural History:** 99tl

Additional photography by Andy Crawford: 71ct, 82-83 (*Trooden* models), 88tc, 89tr, 105tl

Jacket images: Back: Corbis: Louie Psihoyos tl; **DK Images:** Luis Rey tc

All other images © Dorling Kindersley
For further information see: www.dkimages.com

Acknowledgments

Dorling Kindersley would like to thank:
Tim Lott at The Dinosaur Museum, Dorchester, England, (www.thedinosaurmuseum.com) for all his help, Penny Smith, Fleur Star, Lorrie Mack, and Carrie Love for editorial assistance and Gemma Fletcher and Hedi Gutt for design assistance.

Eoraptor, a turkey-sized dinosaur that lived in the Triassic period.